T0113651

A PLUME BOOK

THE MEANING OF MATTHEW

JUDY SHEPARD is cofounder with her husband, Dennis, of the Matthew Shepard Foundation, which is dedicated to her son's legacy. The foundation is committed to the causes championed by Matthew during his life: social justice; diversity awareness and education; and equality for gay, lesbian, bisexual, and transgender people. Doing her part, Judy Shepard speaks around the country to a wide variety of audiences on behalf of the foundation in order to promote tolerance and curb prejudice.

Praise for *The Meaning of Matthew*

"[This] towers over the majority of books written about high-profile issues and events. . . . Judy Shepard is one woman telling one story—which she does with eloquence and heart."   —*Chicago Sun-Times*

"Honest, brave, and beautiful! This book breaks your heart. It is as much Matthew's story as it is the story of a woman's awakening to her position and power in history, as a mother, as a human rights activist, as a citizen. And it's told with the clarity and no-nonsense wisdom that have become Judy's trademarks."

—Moisés Kaufman, author with the members of
Tectonic Theater Project of *The Laramie Project*

"In this extraordinary volume, a courageous, eloquent, and devoted mother tells the world the deeply moving story of her son, Matthew Shepard, whose tragic death in 1998 shocked the conscience of our country. Ever since that horrible hate crime, Judy Shepard has dedicated her own life to promoting tolerance and understanding. Now, in her own beautiful words, Judy gives us all a greater understanding of Matthew and the larger meaning of his life. In doing so, she demonstrates the difference that each individual can make in achieving a better and more just society. She's a true profile in courage, and America will be a fairer nation because of her."   —Senator Edward M. Kennedy

"*The Meaning of Matthew* is Judy Shepard's passionate and courageous attempt to understand what no mother should have to understand, which is why her son was murdered in Laramie, Wyoming, in the fall of 1998. It is a vivid testimony to a life cut short, and testimony, too, to the bravery and compassion of Judy and Dennis—Matthew's parents—as they struggle to survive a grief that won't go away."
—Larry McMurtry, author of *Terms of Endearment* and *Lonesome Dove*

THE MEANING OF

Matthew

My Son's Murder in Laramie,
and a World Transformed

JUDY SHEPARD

WITH JON BARRETT

A PLUME BOOK

PLUME
Published by the Penguin Group
Penguin Group (USA) Inc., 375 Hudson Street, New York, New York 10014, U.S.A. • Penguin
Group (Canada), 90 Eglinton Avenue East, Suite 700, Toronto, Ontario, Canada M4P 2Y3 (a
division of Pearson Penguin Canada Inc.) • Penguin Books Ltd., 80 Strand, London WC2R
0RL, England • Penguin Ireland, 25 St. Stephen's Green, Dublin 2, Ireland (a division of
Penguin Books Ltd.) • Penguin Group (Australia), 250 Camberwell Road, Camberwell,
Victoria 3124, Australia (a division of Pearson Australia Group Pty. Ltd.) • Penguin Books
India Pvt. Ltd., 11 Community Centre, Panchsheel Park, New Delhi – 110 017, India •
Penguin Group (NZ), 67 Apollo Drive, Rosedale, North Shore 0632, New Zealand (a division
of Pearson New Zealand Ltd.) • Penguin Books (South Africa) (Pty.) Ltd., 24 Sturdee Avenue,
Rosebank, Johannesburg 2196, South Africa

Penguin Books Ltd., Registered Offices: 80 Strand, London WC2R 0RL, England

Published by Plume, a member of Penguin Group (USA) Inc. Previously published in a
Hudson Street Press edition.

First Plume Printing, June 2010

Ⓟ REGISTERED TRADEMARK—MARCA REGISTRADA

The Library of Congress has catalogued the Hudson Street Press edition as follows:

Shepard, Judy.
    The meaning of Matthew : my son's murder in Laramie, and a world transformed/Judy
Shepard with Jon Barrett.
    p.   cm.
  ISBN 978-1-59463-057-6 (hc.)
  ISBN 978-0-452-29638-1 (pbk.)
1. Shepard, Matthew, d 1998—Death and burial. 2. Gay men—Crimes against—Wyoming—
Laramie. 3. Homicide—Wyoming—Laramie. 4. Laramie (Wyo.)—Social conditions—20th
century. 5. Shepard, Judy. 6. Shepard, Matthew, d. 1998—Family. 7. Mothers and sons—United
States. 8. Children—United States—Death. 9. Loss (Psychology) 10. Gay rights—United States.
I. Barrett, Jon. II. Title.
  HV6250.4H66S54   2009
  364.152'3092—dc22   2009013512

Set in Janson Text

*Penguin is committed to publishing works of quality and integrity.
In that spirit, we are proud to offer this book to our readers;
however, the story, the experiences, and the words
are the author's alone.*

146122990

This story is dedicated to all the "Matts" out there who feel that Matt's story is a reflection of their own struggle. Hope is out there and change is coming.

Foreword

J UDY SHEPARD AND I first spoke to each other in early 2006, when she called to say how much she admired the film *Brokeback Mountain*. (I should confess that we have never met in person.) During that introductory conversation, we talked about other things, too, things like the vicissitudes of motherhood, and the singular tragedy of losing a child, a tragedy we had both experienced. We spoke for only a short time, but Judy's easy warmth and quiet strength made me feel as if I had known her for years. Before we said good-bye, Judy told me about her desire to write a book someday: a book about her son, Matthew.

I became aware of Matthew Shepard the evening of October 8, 1998, when my daughter Sara phoned from Laramie, Wyoming—she was attending the university there on a basketball scholarship—to tell me that a fellow student, a young man, had been discovered tied to a fence, unconscious and severely beaten, less than a half mile from where she lived at the time. Once Sara learned that the young man, Matthew, was listed in critical condition at a nearby hospital, she decided to ask the university's athletic director to hold a moment of silence for Matthew at the weekend football game. When the athletic director replied that questions had been raised about the nature of the attack and whether the victim was gay, Sara was adamant: Matthew was a University of Wyoming student who had been brutally attacked, and he deserved the unconditional support of the university and its student body.

I had already made plans to be in Laramie for Sara's birthday, and so I arrived there Friday evening, October 9. We did our best to avoid the media frenzy in town. I attended Sara's basketball practices and went with her to some of her classes. We had a leisurely picnic with Annie Proulx up on the Medicine Bow.

I remember that the moment of silence was held for Matthew before the University of Wyoming's football game on Saturday; I remember that Sara and I wept when we learned that Matthew had passed away.

A few weeks ago, Judy Shepard sent me an early manuscript of *The Meaning of Matthew*.

Her book is amazing. And so is she.

Diana Ossana
March 20, 2009

Acknowledgments

Our journey since October 1998 has been very difficult. We have survived because of several people who came into our lives when we needed them most. Many of them have been acknowledged in the body of the book. I'm taking this additional opportunity to give special thanks to a few other very important individuals and organizations.

While in Laramie awaiting both trials, we were house-guests of a generous man who wanted to protect us from the prying eyes of the media. He wishes to remain anonymous, but I want to thank him.

Matt's friend and high school adviser, Cynthia, came to Laramie to be with me for the trial of Aaron McKinney. That meant so much to me, especially since Dennis couldn't be there for the beginning of the proceedings.

Thank you to David Smith from the Human Rights Campaign (HRC), who also came to Laramie to be with us for McKinney's trial. Thank you to Joan Garry and Cathy Renna, who were then part of the Gay and Lesbian Alliance Against Defamation (GLAAD), and were responsible for educating the media in general about the gay community and fairness in reporting. Thank you to Jim Anderson, formerly of the Gay, Lesbian, and Straight Education Network (GLSEN), for his inspired work with that organization and for his friendship. Thank you to fellow board members of HRC, Terry Bean, Vic Basile, Bruce Bastian, John Sullivan, and Mike Berman, for their friendship as well as their patient tutoring of someone new to the world of activism.

The president of the University of Wyoming at the time of Matt's death, Phil Dubois, and the vice president of student affairs, Jim Hurst, are examples of how an administration should respond to the needs of their students, faculty, and staff in similar situations. Their professionalism and empathy were extraordinary.

We will be forever grateful to the lead investigator for the Albany County Sheriff's Department, Rob DeBree, and the lead investigator for the City of Laramie Police Department, Dave O'Malley, for their continued compassion, understanding, and activism. Both departments as a whole were kind and professional. We were very fortunate to have such caring people working to solve Matt's murder and prosecute his murderers.

Thank you to Moisés Kaufman and the Tectonic Theater Project for their brilliant and transformative work, *The Laramie Project*.

Acknowledgments

Thank you to friends Nancy Rauchfuss, Kathy Browning, Randi Driscoll, and Cyndi Lauper. They have helped me in ways too many to list.

In May 1999, Sir Elton John came to Laramie, Wyoming, to acknowledge all the wonderful people who live in Wyoming. He felt that they had been wrongfully maligned by others who blamed them for Matt's death. He gave a benefit concert that was a healing and cathartic event for all of us—an event that is still talked about out of respect for Sir Elton's generous spirit and tremendous talent. His generous spirit and tremendous talent came back to Laramie in April 2009. Again, the experience was overwhelming and indescribable. Thank you.

Author's Note

MEMORIES CAN BE TRICKY. They are often influenced by an individual's life experiences both before and after any event. I have tried to verify my memories with trial transcripts and other written materials as well as conversations with those involved in the memories themselves. There may be some things that are remembered differently by others, but I have put my truth on these pages.

You knew him as Matthew. To us he was Matt. I have tried to reconcile the two within these pages. It would be unfair to Matt if only Matthew's story was told. Matt was so much more than "Matthew Shepard, the gay twenty-one-year-old University of Wyoming college student." He had a family and countless friends. He had a life before the night he was tied to that fence.

THE MEANING OF
Matthew

CHAPTER

One

I<small>T'S OFTEN SAID</small> that we see a white light before we die. I wonder if that is what Matt saw that last night of his consciousness or if the last thing he saw was Aaron McKinney's hateful face.

A <small>PHONE CALL WOKE</small> me with a jolt at about 5:00 a.m. on Thursday, October 8, 1998. My husband, Dennis, and I were living in Dhahran, Saudi Arabia, where he worked as a construction safety manager. I assumed that the call was from my twenty-one-year-old son, Matt, who was living in Laramie and studying political science and international relations at the University of Wyoming. At that time of day, it was almost always him. Unlike our other family and friends in the States, who usually calculated the nine-hour time difference between Wyoming and Saudi Arabia before dialing, Matt always seemed to be living in the moment and wanted to share things with someone right now, regardless of what time it was anywhere else. Or maybe he thought it was just too much math to work out the difference.

Sometimes he'd telephone to talk about a new friend he'd just met at a coffee shop—Matt loved to bend a stranger's ear over a cup of coffee. Other times he'd want to get my opinion on something in the news or alert me to a breaking story. "Did you hear what just happened to Princess Diana? She's dead!" he'd blurted when I picked up the telephone a little more than a year before.

Not that I didn't understand, and appreciate, the impulse. Matt and I were incredibly close; so much so that at times it seemed like we were feeding off each other's energy. I always felt that the normal bond between mother and child was for some reason stronger between us—perhaps because we depended so much on each other for company when Matt was a colicky baby, when I was a fledgling parent and Dennis always seemed to be on the road for work.

Now that Matt was an adult and he and I were living continents and oceans away from each other, our conversations were shorter than I would have wished (at five dollars a minute they had to be) and more spread apart than they used to be. But when he did make those early morning or late-night calls, the joy I felt from hearing his voice more than made up for any resulting loss of sleep.

But the phone call that Thursday morning wasn't from Matt. It was about him. When the man on the other end of the line announced who he was, an emergency room doctor from Ivinson Memorial Hospital in Laramie, I went numb.

I don't remember what he said, or what I did next. I'm not sure whether it was the ringing phone or my subsequent gasp that startled the still-sleeping Dennis. Whatever it was that woke him, Dennis took the phone from me and then, after a seemingly endless silence, made a noise—a sort of helpless and mournful groan—that I'd never heard before and haven't heard since. Coming as it did from my husband, a man whose reserved manner is as typically masculine and western as his Wrangler jeans and cowboy boots, the moan confirmed my worst fears.

Matt had been attacked. He had sustained injuries to his head that were so critical his chances for survival were nearly impossible.

"In fact," Dr. Cantway told Dennis, "Matt's wounds are so severe that he had to be transported forty miles south of Laramie, to a hospital in Fort Collins, Colorado, that was better equipped to deal with head injuries."

As short as the call was—not more than five minutes—it was long enough, not only to turn our world upside down, but to send it spinning forever in the opposite direction. As I remember it, neither Dennis nor I had much to say to the doctor—or to each other. But we were dizzy with questions: Who? Where? Why? What? And most important, how was Matt? But Dr. Cantway couldn't answer anything we asked—other than to say that things didn't look good and that the only piece of information the police had found so far was Matt's

University of Wyoming ID card. Thankfully, that card led them to his emergency contact, Matt's godmother, who worked as a nurse at Ivinson and had our contact information. The hospital called us immediately after getting our Saudi Arabian telephone number.

The rest of that morning was a blur. I do remember thinking, "If I come apart now, I'm never going to make it." Dennis and I were in shock and sort of went into autopilot, knowing there were things we needed to accomplish before we could give in to our fears.

Like all parents, our first instinct was to run to our son's side. Unfortunately, we happened to be eight thousand miles away. The flight to Denver, by way of Amsterdam and Minneapolis, didn't leave for nineteen hours. To add to the already surreal situation, we still had to deal with the bureaucracy of Saudi Arabia and get the proper documentation to leave. Dennis and I were forced to wait almost an entire day before we could even begin our trip to be with Matt. We used that time to call a few relatives in the States to let them know what was happening and to make sure Matt wouldn't be alone in Fort Collins. None of us knew what we'd find or would have to do once we reached Colorado.

As Dennis and I rushed around in a daze—packing our bags and preparing paperwork rather than staring at the slow-moving clock—I did everything I could to stay hopeful. Dennis and I only had limited information about the extent of

Matt's injuries, and absolutely no information about the circumstances surrounding his attack. We knew he was critically injured and that his hold on life was tenuous, at best. Still, our highest hope at that point was for Matt's complete recovery. Our most basic, and perhaps most realistic, hope was that he would hold on to life until we could be with him, by his side.

During the nineteen hours that Dennis and I waited in Dhahran, we were in constant contact with Ivinson Hospital and then Poudre Valley Hospital. But in all that time, there was very little they could tell us about what had happened to Matt. Although the medical staff knew Matt had been attacked—his injuries were too severe to suggest anything else—nobody could explain who had done this to my son or why. When it came down to it, I knew that no amount of speculation on my part would help answer any of the thousands of questions that were already overwhelming me. Even if I could find answers, I knew that none would ease the panic or the excruciating pain welling up at the root of my soul. No answer could help Matt, who was hanging on to life with every ounce of his incredible strength. So as our plane finally took off, for the first leg of our long flight, I gripped Dennis's hand and tried to force myself to think of better times.

CHAPTER

Two

THINKING OF BETTER TIMES, for me, included going all the way back to my teenage years in Glenrock, Wyoming, a quiet town about twenty miles east of Casper along Highway 25. Glenrock's the kind of place parents think is great for raising children, and, at the same time, the kind of place kids can't wait to escape as soon as they're old enough to do so. It's a tiny town—only about fifteen hundred people lived there when I was growing up, and there are maybe an additional eight hundred residents today. According to local legend, Glenrock is where Wyoming's first Christmas was celebrated—at a Pony Express station back in 1859. But beyond that one holy night, Glenrock was just the kind of place where nothing ever seemed to happen.

My family had been in town for years before I was born, in 1952. My dad, Frances Peck, was the town postmaster, and my mom, Vera, was one of his three employees. Since Glenrock wasn't big enough to have home postal delivery, everybody in town had to go to the post office to pick up their mail. As a result, my parents knew everyone and everything, which also meant they knew every little thing I was ever up to.

I wasn't really a wild child; though once I was in high school I did attend my fair share of keggers along the Platte River, on the north side of town. For the most part, my after-school activities centered on the traditionally tame activities of student government, National Honor Society, pep squad, and Job's Daughters. You pretty much have to be involved in everything when your graduating class is only twenty-seven strong and the entire high school population is one hundred.

When I wasn't at school, I spent a lot of time alone at home. Because my sister and brother, Kay and Jim, were fifteen and sixteen years older than me, I always felt like I was an only child. My mom was thirty-nine when I was born, and my dad was forty-four, making me the proverbial menopause baby. There was never any question in my mind that my folks loved me, but by the time I was born they had their own social lives very well established. When they weren't at the post office, Mom and Dad always seemed to be at a function, either social or civic. I suppose I would have been considered a latchkey kid if it weren't for the fact that nobody in Glenrock ever locked their front door. Maybe that's why I live so much in my head today. Sometimes I find it very difficult and, at times, incredibly uncomfortable to express my feelings or show my emotions, whether it's to a roomful of strangers or a handful of friends. I don't want sympathy or pity, and I definitely don't like drawing attention to myself. So, as much as I can help it, I usually wait until no one else is around before I allow myself to think about anything that might make me cry. Soul-searching, heartbreaking memories, and my grief are all very private affairs for me.

There's no denying that my friends and I lived a simple life in Glenrock when we were growing up. When it came right down to it, I don't think we were expected to do much more than graduate from high school, maybe go to college, get married, and then live in Glenrock for the rest of our lives. Despite that simplicity—or perhaps because of it—my hometown still represents everything I've grown to love about Wyoming. The people there were honest, straightforward, and without any pretense whatsoever. Growing up there meant that I was surrounded by a level of acceptance that's hard to find in a larger city—whether it's Cheyenne or Chicago, Denver or New York. I think that's because in small towns you can't help but know everyone else around you. And while you might not always agree with all your neighbors, or even fully understand their eccentricities, you accept them as integral parts of your community.

Glenrock also represents everything I miss about Wyoming when I'm away. Sure, the winters are brutal—I don't think I'll ever get nostalgic about scraping ice off the windshield as the harshest wind in the Lower 48 freezes my face and hands. But after those winds die down and the sun finally shines—whether it's in spring, summer, fall, or winter—I've never seen a brighter, bluer sky. Sometimes when I'm trapped in a canyon of skyscrapers or stuck on the employee compound in Saudi Arabia, I comfort myself with memories of the Wyoming sky—the big sky—and how, when I'm home, no matter where I stand I can almost always see the blue meet the horizon.

However, by the time my high school graduation came around I was like every other eighteen-year-old in town, itching to get away from my parents and dying to see the outside world. I couldn't wait to get out of Glenrock.

I didn't get very far though. I'd been accepted to several out-of-state colleges, but none of those offers came with scholarship money. We couldn't afford to pay for anything more expensive than in-state tuition, so I enrolled at the University of Wyoming in Laramie. It's only about two and a half hours southwest of Glenrock, but I was definitely a world away from everything I knew.

When I started classes, I thought I wanted to be a pharmacist, but then I realized that pharmacy school required a five-year commitment and that was more than I was willing to give. So I ended up just taking courses that caught my interest, mostly in history and literature. When it came time to declare my major, I worked with my adviser to mold one that would best fit that course load. I ended up majoring in education, with an emphasis in high school social studies.

I'd been on campus for a little more than a year before I first noticed Dennis Shepard, a recent graduate from the College of Education and a member of the Phi Delta Theta fraternity, where I was a Little Sister. He lived forty-five miles away, in Cheyenne, where he was working in the newly established Wyoming Occupational Health and Safety Department, but he drove to Laramie almost every weekend to party with his fraternity brothers.

What first struck me about Dennis was that he looked just like my movie idol, Steve McQueen. Hello? Who wouldn't notice a guy who looked like that? But as striking as I thought he was, I never considered Dennis much more than a passing fancy. He seemed stuck-up—and all the girls in my dorm said he was a player, a "love 'em and leave 'em" kind of guy. I had no interest in anybody like that—no matter how much he looked like a movie star.

At Christmas, though, the guys at Phi Delta Theta were throwing a party that I didn't want to attend without a date. So when a common friend of Dennis's and mine offered to set us up for the party, I was more than willing to go along with his plan. When my girlfriends heard what I was up to, they repeated the same warnings they'd shared when I first saw Dennis on campus: "Don't date him, he's a cheat," and "That guy breaks all the girls' hearts." That's probably why I went into the evening with absolutely no expectations. I thought that I'd get to go to the party of the season with an undeniably handsome guy on my arm; if he turned out to be a complete jerk and we never spoke to each other again, so be it.

But as the night progressed, it became more and more evident how wrong my girlfriends had been about this handsome man. Although Dennis came across as a bit stoic at first (perhaps that's why I thought he was stuck-up), he ended up being funny, charming, and quite the gentleman. At the end of the night, when he took me home, the guy I thought I'd have to fight off didn't even try to kiss me good night. That alone was very impressive.

I can't speak for Dennis, but I never dated anybody else after that night. We were engaged nine months later, when he proposed to me while I was washing dishes, which is more romantic than it sounds. We were married eight months after that, on May 5, 1973, at St. Matthew's Episcopal Cathedral in Laramie.

If the only thing you knew about Dennis was that he was born in Scottsbluff, Nebraska, a city of about fifteen thousand residents, located just east of the Wyoming border, you might assume that he and I had similar upbringings. But while I was the youngest of three children, Dennis was the oldest of five. While my parents were married for sixty-two years, Dennis's folks divorced when he was a young boy. While I spent the whole of my first eighteen years in Glenrock, Dennis moved dozens of times and lived in several states (Nebraska, Oklahoma, California, Idaho twice, and Wyoming three times) before he left home to attend college in Laramie.

Those moves started early as Dennis's father, Harry, a World War II veteran, went where work was available. When Dennis's folks divorced, Harry took custody of the five kids. Since Harry, a union millwright, was always working, much of the care for the family fell first to Harry's sister and her family and then, later, to Dennis. As a result, Dennis seemed to grow up too quickly himself.

When Dennis was about twelve or thirteen, his father married Ruth Stahla, who had actually gone to grade school with Harry in western Nebraska. I firmly believe Ruth saved the Shepard family. She put structure back into everyone's life and, by convincing Harry to finally settle in Cheyenne, put a stop to the family's constant moves back and forth across the western half of the United States.

After graduating from Cheyenne's East High School in 1967, Dennis spent summers working in the Montana oil fields, in the Wyoming trona mines, and on construction projects to pay for tuition, books, and housing. During the school year, he worked in the university cafeteria and his fraternity kitchen for meals and additional money to supplement his college loans and summer wages. Dennis always claimed that his parents spied on him because "care packages" of food and some small amounts of money seemed to show up when he needed them the most, usually near the end of the month.

Immediately upon earning his bachelor's degree in 1972, Dennis took a job with the state's Occupational Safety and Health Administration that required him to be away from home 75 percent of the time. He hasn't slowed down since.

Our courtship was quick, but one of the many things Dennis and I had a chance to talk through before getting married was whether we wanted children. The consensus was that we didn't. This wasn't because either of us was actually opposed to having kids. As I remember it, we both just kind of bought into the theory of the day: There were already too many children in the world, and between Vietnam and the ever-present threat of nuclear war it seemed like only a crazy person would want to add to that number. So I was a little surprised, but not at all disappointed, when after two years of marriage Dennis came home from work one day, put his arms around me, and announced, "I'm twenty-eight now, and if we're going to have a family, I think we better get started." I went off the pill immediately and was pregnant within a few months.

It was a surprisingly easy pregnancy, too. I gained forty-five pounds, which was a lot for my five-foot three-inch frame, but I was lucky and never suffered from morning sickness. Eight months in, I felt so good that I accompanied Dennis and his folks on their annual two-week elk and moose hunting trip to Big Piney, on the western side of Wyoming. I didn't actually hunt—I happily hung around camp, fished for brook trout, and helped out with the cooking instead.

Three

I WAS SUPPOSED TO HAVE a Christmas baby, but my water broke early on the morning of November 30. Dennis was out of town with work, so I drove myself to the hospital, honestly thinking that I'd be sent back home to wait for actual labor to start. But the nurse took one look at me and said, "You're not going anywhere."

As simple as the pregnancy was, the delivery was anything but easy. I was in labor for nearly forty hours, which was sheer hell for me but gave Dennis plenty of time to make it to my side (even though he had to drive through a treacherous Wyoming snowstorm to do so). Finally the doctor decided to perform a Cesarean section, and Matthew Wayne Shepard was born on the afternoon of December 1, 1976. We chose the name Matthew simply because we liked it and Wayne because it is Dennis's middle name.

I was so tired and medicated from the delivery that the birth itself was a blur. In fact, it wasn't until two days after Matt was born that I was conscious enough to remember holding my newborn baby boy, with his muddy blue eyes and blond peach-fuzz hair, for the first time. He was so tiny: under five pounds. But I thought at the time, and still think now, that his size had more to do with genetics than with being born three weeks early.

Aside from the C-section, a number of things with Matt's birth seemed to go wrong right away. First off, we discovered that Matt had jaundice, a condition caused by high levels of bilirubin in the blood, which, if left untreated, can cause brain damage. I found out later that jaundice is a fairly typical condition for newborn babies, but it nevertheless meant that Matt had to stay in the hospital for a week after I went home. Leaving my baby at the hospital felt completely unnatural. It triggered a pretty severe postpartum depression that stretched on for about four months.

It didn't help that once we were finally able to bring Matt home, he was a very cranky baby: colicky and unable to sleep for longer than a couple hours. At the time, I chalked my son's sour temper up to his sour stomach. We found out that he was allergic to milk, a condition that was only exacerbated by a digestive system that seemed to reject anything I fed him by spitting it all up. Looking back now, I'm sure that at least part of Matt's irritable disposition had to do with me—he must have picked up on my mood as I moped around the house uncertain about how this seemingly unhappy baby boy was going to figure into the rest of my life.

Matt didn't take his first steps until he was nearly eighteen months old because he preferred sitting and scooting around the house in his bouncy walker. He took his time learning to speak, too, even though he talked nonstop once he finally did learn to put words together. Matt and I spent so much time alone while Dennis was away at work that we developed a sort of symbiotic relationship where, even after he could talk, speaking didn't seem necessary. Instead we communicated through play and reading books. He loved *Where the Wild Things Are*, the Berenstain Bears series, and anything by Dr. Seuss.

As a small child, Matt used to go through monthlong periods where he'd eat only one thing, such as hot dogs or peanut butter and jelly sandwiches. It still makes me laugh today to remember one time when he was about three and going through a macaroni-and-cheese phase. At the time, NBC was broadcasting the miniseries *Shogun*, which starred Richard Chamberlain and, in those days before cable TV, was a pretty big media event. Every night Matt and I would gather in the living room—me on the sofa and he on his spring-loaded rocking horse. He'd rock the horse while balancing a bowl of macaroni and cheese and brandishing a broomstick turned sword, as if he were a Japanese samurai eating his last meal.

I'm not sure which came first, his interest in TV or his fascination with playacting and dressing up. He loved it all. Some of my favorite photos are of Matt in my curlers and Matt in his father's cowboy hats, baseball hats, and hard hats.

Like many other firstborn children, Matt liked to be with adults, and he liked to be the center of attention. As a result, he grew up to be quite a ham. So much so that after I learned that I was pregnant again, when Matt was nearly four, one of my first thoughts—after the initial elation—was about how Matt would respond to having to share the spotlight with a sibling.

Unlike my pregnancy with Matt, I was sick nearly every day I carried Logan, and I had to go on medication in order to feel even halfway normal. Not that Matt would have noticed any difference in me during those nine months. He was too young, of course, to make sense of any of the changes he might have seen. I do remember, though, that Dennis and I tried to explain that my expanding belly meant that Matt would soon be a big brother. I think he understood. He seemed excited about the prospect of having a baby brother or sister.

Compared to my first experience giving birth, delivering Logan was really easy. It required another C-section, but I was prepared for surgery this time. Once he was born, Logan was a textbook baby. He didn't have to go through the treatment for jaundice and he didn't have any allergies. He was so strong that he was able to turn himself over in the crib the first day I brought him home. Better yet, he slept through the night. As a baby, Logan was everything Matt hadn't been.

Still, I don't think Logan was quite what his older brother expected. Logan was definitely not a puppy. I think Matt was a little reluctant to share the attention that had, just days before, all been his. I never saw it, but Matt later told me that when Logan started to crawl, he often intentionally stepped on his fingers to make him cry or would push his hands out from under him so Logan would fall. Matt would often tease Logan, reminding him that he was supposed to be the library because the room that was now Logan's was originally meant to be a library. I think that particular joke lasted as long as Matt was in our lives.

For all those pranks, there was no denying that Matt eventually developed a soft spot for his little brother. When Logan was around ten, Dennis and I came home after a night out and found a note from Matt on the stairway. In it he reminded us that the following day was Easter Sunday, and then he added, "I hope you remember to get something for Logan because he still expects the Easter Bunny to come and leave presents." We had already colored Easter eggs the night before and bought all the traditional Easter candy but hadn't planned on buying Logan a gift from the Easter Bunny, so Matt really saved us. And to this day I'm amazed by Matt's ability, at such a young age, to anticipate and convey his brother's expectations.

Matt's love for being the center of attention never came at the expense of the needs of the people around him. In fact, even as a child he had an amazing ability to tap into other people's emotions. One Christmas—I think it was probably around 1983—when my folks were staying with us, Matt climbed up on my mom's lap and said, "Grandma?

Did something happen? Do you feel bad? You don't look happy."

I don't know what was bugging my mom that day, she was probably just tired, but she turned to me and asked, "How can he tell? How does this seven-year-old know how I feel? How can he be so empathetic?" Of course, I didn't have an answer for her. Matt just seemed to be more sensitive to people's feelings than other kids his age.

When Matt was a couple of years older and got to know some of our neighbors, he started trying to lift their spirits by writing little poems and illustrating them with stick-figure drawings. He then left the drawings in different mailboxes along the street. It was probably my dad, the postmaster, who broke it to little Matt that it was illegal to put unauthorized mail in people's boxes. So Matt decided to leave pretty rocks in their mailboxes instead.

Years later Matt was voted a peer counselor at his high school, which meant that he had been selected by his peers as a person that kids in his class could talk to about issues they weren't comfortable sharing with an adult. As anyone who knew him would have guessed, Matt was a natural at the job. His high school friends later told me that the best thing about talking with Matt was the way he made everyone feel that they were the only ones in the world at that moment—that he was focused entirely on them, that he really listened to them. My mother had told Matt, "The Lord gave us two ears and one mouth for a reason. We need to listen twice as much as we need to talk." I guess Matt took that to heart.

The only trouble was that Matt couldn't seem to separate his classmates' problems from his own life. He absorbed everything he heard and became sad for his friends, endlessly worrying about them, and crying for them from time to time, especially when he had no solution to offer. Matt told me one night that he might want to become a psychologist, and I remember asking, "How can you do that, Matt? You're going to first have to figure out a way to build a wall between other people's problems and your own."

One of the outlets my sensitive little boy found for all these overwhelming emotions was the stage. He started acting in elementary school—Dennis and I still treasure the video footage of him playing the part of Abraham Lincoln, decked out in shorts and a stovepipe hat made of construction paper, at his sixth-grade history day. He was also one of the youngest-ever members of Casper's community theater group, Stage III, and was cast in a number of productions at Casper College. He played the role of the little brother in Casper College's production of Thornton Wilder's *Our Town*, was part of the chorus when the college staged *The Music Man*, and had one of the leading roles in Stage III's production of a Kurt Vonnegut play called *Happy Birthday, Wanda June*. He was also an active crew member, working backstage on many shows, which led me to believe that his interest in theater—especially in the community and college-level productions—was less about the glory associated with being onstage than it was about being part of a creative venture.

Matt also started getting involved in politics at seven years old, stuffing envelopes for a local candidate and campaigning for an environmental group that was working to get the city of Casper to start a recycling program. Matt was markedly shorter and thinner than almost any of the boys his age, but he was growing up to be a very astute and adultlike thinker. When presented with the option, he seemed to prefer the company of adults over that of his peers.

Not that there weren't always plenty of children around our neighborhood. Before I found out I was pregnant with Logan, Dennis and I moved the family to a two-level home in a brand-new subdivision on the west side of Casper called Sunrise Addition. The new neighborhood had been built in response to the town's exploding population.

Ever since the energy crisis of the 1970s, the oil business in Wyoming had been booming, and people were moving into the state, and our city, in droves. As a result, Casper was practically a company town. All the families who moved there were young, most had moved when we did, almost everyone worked in the same industry, and nearly all the homes had young children about Matt's and Logan's ages. The kids were always getting together to play laser tag and hide-and-seek. We had one of the few homes in the neighborhood with a flat driveway, which made our house the best spot for basketball, skate-boarding, and Big Wheel riding, so most of the neighborhood kids usually gathered right outside our front door. We all felt so safe then. We always knew where our children were. If they weren't in our yard, they were undoubtedly at someone else's house in the neighborhood.

Nearly every summer, usually when Dennis's folks were visiting from Arizona, our family would pack up the truck and go camping in the mountains of eastern Wyoming near Big Piney. The boys loved to fish, and we'd often eat the previous day's catch for breakfast. Matt was more of a catch-and-release kind of fisherman, like his mother, because he didn't want to have to gut and clean the fish. He may have felt differently if there were showers at the campground, but he hated to go to bed with fish guts under his fingernails. Matt simply preferred to leave the dirty work to his grand-father or Dennis.

Come fall, Dennis and his dad would often take the boys bird hunting (usually for blue grouse, sage chicken, or dove). One year he even took them out moose hunting; the boys look so proud in the photos from that trip, with their moose loaded in the back of the truck. The only complaint the boys had was that Dennis still made them do their homework.

It's nearly impossible not to feel nostalgic for those days when the boys and their friends would spend all day right out-side the front door, and when we'd spend so many summer nights counting all the stars we could see from our backyard. Thinking about those times today, it seems as if Dennis and I didn't have a care in the world. I know it's a bit cliché to say it, but things really were much simpler back then.

In fact, one of the only concerns I remember having in regard to the boys shouldn't, in retrospect, really have been much of a worry at all: I had the beginnings of a notion that Matt might be gay. It's difficult to pinpoint exactly when this thought first crossed my mind. When people ask me about it today, I usually say that I figured it out when Matt was in elementary school and dressed up as Dolly Parton for Halloween two years in a row. But then someone who heard me tell that story sent me an e-mail accusing me of perpetuating stereotypes. I suppose I can see why someone might think that—there are many straight men out there who were fascinated with Dolly Parton when they were boys. But I suspect those boys may have been interested in Dolly for reasons different from Matt's.

I guess I started to question that Matt was somehow different even before he went to elementary school—probably when he was as young as three or four years old and in preschool. I started asking myself why my little boy was so sensitive to other people's issues—why he cared so much about things most kids never even thought of. Even in preschool, Matt took it personally when his friends wouldn't share with each other. He hated it when one kid teased or was mean to another. At the time, though, I didn't have enough life experience to be able to connect the dots.

When I was growing up in Glenrock, I didn't know anyone who was gay (or at least I didn't know that I did). The very concept of "gay" was something I never really thought about—and I don't think the people around me thought about it either. It simply wasn't on anybody's radar. That changed a little bit when I moved to Laramie to go to college and realized there were a few gay people on campus. But even then, there wasn't any real acknowledgment among my peers that these people were gay; nobody ever talked about it. Most of us just knew there were women on campus who dated other women, and we accepted that as the case without really thinking much about it.

Now, that's not to say that people weren't homophobic in Wyoming back then. I think they probably were—and would have showed it if they had any real consciousness of gay people. I also don't think that made Wyoming any different from the rest of the country. I'd be willing to bet that the reaction, or lack thereof, would have been a lot different if there had been an openly gay male couple on campus. The other guys at the university probably wouldn't have been able to look past the idea of two men together. I imagine that some of the straight guys would have felt like they had to say something—or do something—to assert their own heterosexuality, for whatever reason. But I don't remember even thinking about this while I was a student.

Just like today, back in the 1970s there were a lot of gay slurs thrown around campus. We heard everything from "fag" to "queer" and "sissy." But I don't think I ever heard those words used to describe someone who anyone actually thought was gay. They were instead used as part of hazing in a fraternity, in the athletic department, or simple horsing around. I realize today that it's not okay to use that kind of hateful language in any situation, even if it's simply meant in jest. I truly believe that the people who were talking like that back in the early seventies at the University of Wyoming were doing so out of ignorance rather than any sort of malice.

So my hunch about Matt's sexual orientation was based on my limited experience with gay people, on stereotypes, and, perhaps more important, on a sense I had as a mother of who my son was and who he was growing up to be. It's a sense I still stand by today when talking with and about parents of gay children. I think a mother just knows.

Sixth sense or not, the idea still frightened me a bit. It wasn't that the prospect of having a gay son bothered me for any religious or moral reasons. There was never any question that I'd love Matt as much as ever no matter who he grew up to be or how he did it. But I couldn't help but wonder what being gay would mean for him. So much of the happiness in my life depended on my spouse and my children. Like so many parents who first discover their child is gay—or even contemplate the prospect of having a kid who grows up to be gay—I assumed that Matt would never have a family of his own. I conjured up a grim forecast for my son: a lonely and loveless existence.

I think it was this fear, combined with a real lack of information about gay people, that kept me from mentioning my suspicion about Matt to anyone. It was the early eighties, after all, and my only sources about homosexuality at the time were the media reports about HIV and AIDS, which didn't make me feel any better about the chance that Matt might be growing up gay. I really couldn't expect to find anything in the Casper library, and there weren't (and still aren't) any gay bookstores in Wyoming. I thought that if I couldn't fully understand homosexuality myself, then there was no way I could know for sure if Matt were gay—short of him telling me so. For me, it didn't make sense to discuss my intuition with anyone, not even Dennis. I feared that by doing so I would risk changing the way people felt about and acted around Matt. At the root of it, I think my biggest fear was that people would treat him differently or even hurt him.

Matt was already head and shoulders smaller than the other kids his age, which bothered him more and more as he got older. Although the learning disabilities he had weren't diagnosed yet (it wasn't until Matt was tested in high school that we learned he had attention deficit disorder), it was clear as early as age nine that Matt had difficulty in school. In my mind, life was already throwing enough at Matt without him having to deal with being gay. So I kept my hunches secret, tried to educate myself whenever and however I could, and—as strange as it sounds for me to say this today—hoped that I was wrong.

CHAPTER
Four

THE COLLAPSE OF INTERNATIONAL OIL PRICES in the mid- and late eighties swept jobs away from Wyoming. Between 1984 and 1987, the state lost nearly forty thousand jobs—a number that's even more dramatic when you consider that there were fewer than five hundred thousand people living in the state at the time. In 1986 Dennis lost his job due to a merger. He was hired by another oil company almost right away but was out of work again in 1991 because of another merger. In 1992 he started working in New Mexico and had to be away from the boys and me for months at a time.

By 1993, when Matt was finishing his sophomore year at Natrona County High School, the job market in Wyoming had dried up. It was clear that our family was going to have to move if we wanted to ever spend any time together. Dennis could keep his current job, and we would move to New Mexico, or he could take a second offer, with Saudi Aramco, that would have us moving to Dhahran, Saudi Arabia. I remember

Dennis and I agreed at the time that as long as we were going to have to move, we might as well really move—so we were leaning toward Saudi Arabia. But we were worried about how the boys, and Matt in particular, would feel about the idea. Just like I'd done in Glenrock when I was a kid, Matt and Logan had spent their whole lives in one town, growing up with the same friends. Matt also was very active with his extracurricular activities, which included an impressive list of theatrical productions and several political campaigns. I assumed that the furthest thing from either of my sons' minds—and, honestly, the last thing either would want—would be a move that would take them half a world away from everything and everyone they knew.

But Dennis and I believed our boys would benefit from a total change in scenery—a shift in people's (and their own) expectations of who and what they were supposed to be when they grew up. I also hoped that such a move might especially help Matt. If he was indeed growing up gay, as I suspected more and more every day, he'd need to be in a more open-minded learning environment, one that celebrated individuality. Perhaps it was mother's intuition, but I had a strong sense that Matt was struggling to find an identity, a sense of who he really was. I had a feeling that might be a tricky endeavor in Casper.

Dennis and I couldn't have been more surprised when the boys jumped at the opportunity to move overseas. The biggest selling point, I think, was that Saudi Aramco paid the tuition for employees' high school–age children to attend boarding school anywhere in the world. Boarding school was particularly appealing to Matt. He had already started to toy with the idea of a career in international relations and with that goal in mind, had been taking German in school. Logan was still young enough that he would attend classes in the Saudi Aramco compound. Boarding school seemed a long way off to him.

By the time we finalized our decision and started to make arrangements for the move to Saudi Arabia, we were up against the deadline for signing Matt up for school. As a result, we didn't have time to visit any of the schools that were in the running. Instead we relied on stacks of catalogs and advice from other parents in the compound to narrow our choices down to three. It was between the American schools in England, Greece, and Switzerland. Matt initially had his heart set on a school in Thorpe, England, about eighteen miles southwest of London. But as perfect a setup as it seemed to Matt, Dennis and I were having a little difficulty dealing with the reality of sending our teenage boy to boarding school thousands of miles away. Just months before, an IRA truck bomb had ripped through the center of London, killing forty people, so the United Kingdom didn't seem like the best choice. Neither did the school in Athens, for that matter. Seven years before, a Palestinian splinter group had detonated a bomb on a TWA flight en route there. I'm sure both schools are stellar and that both provide top-notch educations, but considering Dennis's and my skittishness at the time (what loving parents wouldn't feel that way sending their kid to live by himself overseas?), the school in the politically neutral country of Switzerland seemed like our best bet.

After Matt learned about the foreign-language opportunities that would be open to him in Switzerland, where most residents are fluent in several languages, he wasn't so disappointed to be missing out on London or Athens. His new campus would be in Lugano, near the northern border of Italy. The fifty thousand people who live there alternately speak Italian, French, and English. With the German Matt started studying in Casper and the other languages he would pick up from a roommate in Lugano, he could converse in several languages—some more fluently than others. Probably the most impressive thing, at least to Logan, was that he had learned to swear in nearly every language by the time he graduated from high school.

Matt and I did get to visit London anyway. As it turned out, the dress code at his new school—jackets, collared shirts, slacks, and dress shoes—was significantly different from what we were used to in cowboy country. So after moving the family to Saudi Arabia, and before taking Matt to Switzerland, he and I visited the United Kingdom to get a few things for him to wear, while Dennis stayed behind in Saudi Arabia with Logan.

Shopping was much more difficult than either of us expected it would be. Matt was, and always had been, so much smaller than other kids his age. But when he was dressing in T-shirts, jeans, and sneakers, his size didn't seem to matter so much. Big and baggy was in, and Matt didn't mind that he swam in his clothes because everyone else did. But dress clothes were different. Most of the jackets he tried on in London made him look like a kid who was dressing up in his dad's clothes for Halloween. I didn't dare suggest that we scan the boys' section. Matt may have been smaller than average, but his temper was just as big as any teenager's. The last thing I needed was a meltdown in the middle of Harrods department store. It frustrated us both, but it was clearly tougher on him; he was stressed out about making a good impression on his new classmates, and the right clothes were the clearest first step in that process.

Having finally secured a few pieces of the closest-fitting clothes we could find (which we still had to have altered in Switzerland), Matt and I spent the next several days sightseeing. First we hit the West End to see *Phantom of the Opera* and *Les Misérables*, two of the most audience-friendly plays ever written. Knowing all the work that went into pulling off the shows he was involved with in Casper, Matt was awestruck by the power and accomplishment of both productions. We also took Matt's picture in front of the Hard Rock Cafe, went to Madame Tussauds wax museum, toured the Tower of London and Sherlock Holmes's fictional residence at 221b Baker Street, and then strolled through St. James's Park. It was one of those quintessential mother-son bonding times, marked by both the stress of the clothes shopping and the frivolity of the sightseeing. I wouldn't trade that special time with Matt in London for anything.

After England the two of us flew on to Zurich, where we met my brother, Jim, who'd flown over from Wyoming, for a quick tour of Switzerland. We took a day trip to Interlaken, a breathtaking hideaway in the Alps, and enjoyed one of the best meals I've ever had, at the Dolder Grand hotel in Zurich. Before finally heading to Lugano, the three of us loaded up on bread, salami, beer (soda for Matt), and Sprüngli chocolate at the Zurich train station. As our train headed south toward the Italian border, we enjoyed the staggeringly beautiful scenery, passing the snowcapped Alps and crossing a bridge whose name I've never learned but which I have ever since described as "ginormous."

Just south of the Swiss Alps, and perched over Lake Maggiore, the campus for the American School in Switzerland (TASIS) was just as picturesque as it looked in the brochures that Dennis, Matt, and I had pored over. But Matt's face fell when he first saw the residence hall. In the recruiting materials, the school's buildings were described romantically; I remember that one of them had been a mansion owned by the Marchese De Nobili, who, hundreds of years before, had been the Italian ambassador to Switzerland.

While Matt's dorm certainly looked like it had an impressive past, its history was most apparent in the stone steps (which were worn in the center from the centuries of foot traffic), in the dingy bathrooms and showers, and in the castlelike casement windows (that did very little to light the basement dorm room Matt shared with two other boys). The Shepard family had never lived in a mansion or a palace, but this building—for all of its majestic history—was simply cold, dark, and dank. When we first walked in, Matt turned to me with the most sorrowful, desperate look that seemed to cry, "Please don't leave me here!"

Believe me, I didn't want to. I'm sure that's the case for any mother who leaves her child for the first time—whether it's for summer camp, boarding school, or college. It broke my heart. I wanted so much for this to be a good experience for Matt. As enthusiastic as he'd been about going to boarding school when we were all still together in Wyoming, I think the reality of being without his family and in this "alternate universe" hit him like a ton of bricks. I knew that if he went into it thinking he was going to hate it, there was a good chance he'd never really give it much of a shot. And if that happened, his experience was bound to be a miserable one.

Matt was clearly terribly homesick at first. Jim and I stayed in Lugano for a couple of days after we dropped Matt off at school, but the administrators recommended that we have as little contact with him as possible. At their insistence, we didn't visit the campus again during that trip and even refrained from calling to check in with Matt. But that didn't stop him from calling us at the hotel and pleading, "Come and get me! I want to stay with you in the hotel instead of here." I did my best to explain why he couldn't be with us—that he needed to acclimate to this new environment, and that he needed to make new friends—but I don't think anything I said made the separation any easier for Matt or me.

After I left for Saudi Arabia, the distance between us grew wider simply because phone calls between Switzerland and Saudi Arabia were prohibitively expensive. We didn't have e-mail access at the time—it wasn't available yet in the compound or at Matt's school—so we kept in touch by sending each other faxes. Still, it wasn't easy to comfort a homesick kid, or even provide much solace, when communicating over a fax machine.

We did what we could, though, and apparently so did Matt. Within a couple months, the faxes and the phone calls became less frequent. When our fax machine did come to life, the messages Matt sent included stories about the great times he was having with new friends. He even began to speak fondly about his room and how he had decorated it with photos from home. He was going to be okay.

In Wyoming Matt had a few of what might be called best friends, but in Switzerland he made dozens of them. I think there are two kinds of people—those who have really close friends and those who have thousands of acquaintances. Matt always took the time to build strong friendships.

He sought diversity among his peers. As a result, people seemed to seek him out. Whether it was because of his size, or something else less definable that made him come across as vulnerable, a variety of people always tried to give him a hand. Eventually, Matt came to rely on these friends for practical things, like help with his homework and ironing his shirts, and for emotional support as well.

Matt never said, and his friends have never said anything since, but I wouldn't be surprised if Matt at least tiptoed around discussions of sexual orientation with his friends in Lugano— even if he never came out and told them that he thought he might be gay. If he was struggling with the issue at all, as I suspect he was, Matt would have tested the waters to see how people might react, to see if he'd ever be able to come out of the closet.

The biggest difference I noticed in Matt when he came home to Saudi Arabia for the first time was how restless he'd become. He was constantly in search of "something to do," and sitting around on the sofa to watch TV or hanging out with the family wasn't enough. He also seemed to have developed a bit of a temper, flying off the handle (usually at Logan) for what seemed like trivial things. At the time, I chalked it up to being a symptom of simple teenage angst, but it may have been the result of growing pains of a different sort. I imagine that he had to expend so much energy at school, either trying to figure out why he was different from the other students or trying to disguise the fact that he was different, that the only time he could really let down his guard was when he was home with us.

The employee compound in Dhahran was no place for a restless kid like Matt. The compound, just outside the city of al-Khobar, in the eastern province of Saudi Arabia, was too quiet for him. Although the compound houses sixteen thousand people, there is not much there socially for returning students. The business district in al-Khobar was only about a half-hour bus ride away from our home, but it was difficult to shop there because all the stores closed after noontime prayers for three to four hours in the middle of the day, not reopening until evening. I kept busy by cooking and cleaning around the house or by playing mah-jongg or canasta with my friends, but chores and games with his mom's friends had no appeal for Matt.

Thankfully, a classmate of his from TASIS named Zeina also lived on the compound. The two of them were practically joined at the hip—both at school and when they were back home on vacation—constantly spending time together, complaining that there was never "anything to do." But I guess being bored with a friend your own age is much better than being that way with your folks and your kid brother.

It must have been that boredom, combined with a dose of good old-fashioned teenage stupidity and the desire to be a grown-up, that prompted Matt and Zeina to start smoking cigarettes. I freaked out when I first smelled the smoke on Matt's clothes, but he swore up and down that Zeina was the one who was smoking. He just smelled that way because he was hanging out with her. Since I didn't take the initiative to talk with Zeina's parents about her smoking, Matt's explanation sufficed for a couple months—until the night Dennis caught him trying to sneak a smoke in our backyard. Dennis blew his top and read Matt the riot act, preaching to him with a thousand "you should know better's" and then reminding him that I'm allergic to cigarette smoke. "If you want to make yourself sick, go ahead," he lectured, "but I won't let you do it to your mom!" At the time, Matt promised that he'd never smoke again. But unlike in the United States, there were no age restrictions for buying cigarettes in Saudi Arabia or Switzerland. So there was really no way we could keep Matt from smoking. As far as I know, he never did quit. I could only laugh, years later, when I learned that Zeina's parents had a similar freakout upon smelling cigarette smoke on her clothes. She did the same thing Matt did—pleaded innocent and blamed the smell on her friend. But we all know now that our kids were equally guilty of being sneaky and immature.

I'm sure that smoking wasn't the extent of Matt's teenage rebellion. Dennis and I always tried to dissuade both him and Logan from drinking, so while I wouldn't have been surprised if Matt drank in high school, he hid it from me. In addition to those rules, Dennis also prohibited our sons from having any piercings or tattoos while they were "under our roof." In order to avoid his dad's wrath, Matt limited any experiments with his appearance to his hair (which he was constantly changing) and clothes.

WHAT APPEALED TO MATT most about boarding school were the excursions he and the other students took. Trips to Venice, Rome, Florence, and Budapest fed his wanderlust and his growing restlessness. As you might imagine, these journeys gave a kid with dreams of a career in international relations an entirely new perspective on art, culture, and the world around him. Every winter term, the entire TASIS student body and staff spent a month in Saint Moritz, skiing half the day and going to class the other half. Wyoming has some of the best ski hills in the country, but Matt had never had a chance to try them out. So these trips to Saint Moritz were among the most memorable of his school expeditions. Matt, Dennis, Logan, and I had a great laugh about one of Matt's first experiences on skis: He and his classmates were racing down the slope, and Matt was the first to reach the bottom. The only trouble was that it was supposed to be a slalom race, and Matt, who'd never heard the word "slalom," careened straight down the hill rather than zigzagging through the poles.

Matt was particularly excited when, during the second semester of his senior year, school officials allowed the students to take a trip without a chaperone. Most of the kids went to Portugal or Spain—places that Matt considered a little too run-of-the-mill. He wanted to go somewhere a little more exotic and got a group of a dozen or so of his friends to go to Morocco, where they planned to spend a few days in two of the biggest cities, Rabat and Marrakech.

Matt always loved the café culture in Europe, especially relishing the opportunity coffee shops afforded him to meet and talk with the locals. One night, after a full day of sightseeing around Marrakech with his friends, his restlessness got the better of him. After the group returned to the hotel, he realized he wasn't ready to call it a night, so he wandered out alone in search of a café or bar. After sharing a couple of cappuccinos with a group of German tourists, Matt decided to head back to the hotel. But as he worked his way through the ancient city's winding streets, a gang of three local men snuck up behind him and attacked and raped him.

I don't know a lot of the details. Matt never really wanted to share them with me, and I didn't press him to do so. I can't imagine how awful that night must have been for him, and to tell you the truth I don't want to try to imagine it. One of the many things I've learned in the past decade is that when something awful like this happens to someone I love, my most effective coping mechanism is to avoid the temptation to visualize the scene of the crime—to put myself there, to try to understand what happened in my mind's eye. It's bad enough to know that it happened.

By this time Matt was a savvy-enough traveler to know that he was a target for robbery as an American, and he was smart enough to know that he shouldn't go out by himself at night in a strange city. But the three men who targeted Matt that night in Morocco apparently weren't looking to rob him. They left his watch but, for some strange reason, took his shirt and his black Doc Martens. Matt said he fought back, and I have little doubt that he did. I'd never seen him in a physical spat, but I know only a few people with a stronger will than Matt's. Whether he was fighting to prove a point or to save his life, he could be as strong as men twice his size. Still, he was no match for three grown men.

Bloodied, badly beaten, shirtless, and shoeless, he went back to the hotel as soon as he could break free from his attackers and woke up his friends. Since this incident, I've heard many stories about men-on-men gang rapes in Muslim countries where the police were less than helpful in tracking down the perpetrators. In one case reported on by *60 Minutes* in 2007, officials in Dubai actually threatened to charge the fifteen-year-old French-Swiss victim with homosexuality (a charge punishable by death under the strictest interpretation of the Koran) rather than prosecute his three alleged attackers. But Matt met no resistance at the police department in Marrakech. One officer even gave him a picture of a Moroccan on horseback, which was a gesture that really touched Matt and helped him trust that the police not only believed him but were willing to help him out. Still, the Moroccan police never found his attackers.

When Matt called me the following morning to tell me about the attack, he cried and said he was so embarrassed and ashamed. He blamed himself, as so many rape victims do, and couldn't get past the idea that it never would have happened if he hadn't ventured out on his own. Of course, the first thing Dennis and I wanted to do was jump on a plane to be by Matt's side, to make sure he was okay, assure him that he was safe, and tell him over and over again that he wasn't to blame. But to get there, Dennis and I would have had to fly to Amsterdam first to get a connection to Morocco. That would mean Matt would have had to stay in Marrakech longer than any of us wanted him to. Instead the school arranged for a teacher to fly to Morocco to stay with Matt until he could fly home to us.

When Matt finally did get back to Saudi Arabia, about three days after the attack, he underwent a series of physical exams, including an HIV test. Everything checked out okay, and aside from a few cuts, bruises, and scratches he was physically fine. But those three men in Morocco stole more from

Matt that night than his shirt and his shoes. They took his confidence, his optimism, and his sense of purpose and place in the world.

Matt, like any other teenager, had his fair share of insecurities, and maybe a few more, since he was still coming to terms with his sexual orientation. But he was happy and possessed a sense of self before he went to Morocco—always walking upright and sure of himself. After the attack, he seemed to assume the attitude of a beaten-down victim: His posture was slumped, his gait became more of a shuffle, and he purposely chose to wear clothes that were way too big for him, as if he wanted to hide in the fabric.

Matt had loved to act ever since he was a toddler imitating Richard Chamberlain's shogun on his bouncy horse. After the attack in Morocco, he lost all interest in it. "I can't get up on the stage because I feel like everyone's staring at me," he said. "It makes me very uncomfortable."

By far, the most disturbing episodes of the aftermath were the nightmares. He would wake up screaming and drenched in sweat. The psychiatrists we took him to said he was suffering from depression, post-traumatic stress disorder, and anxiety attacks. Each prescribed a number of different drugs, but nothing seemed to really work. It didn't help that Matt hated going to therapy sessions. He used to tell me that he thought the doctors didn't really pay attention to what he was saying. So, before he could trust any of them, Matt would test them by saying whatever crossed his mind, things that were no real reflection of his situation or of how he was feeling. And if the psychiatrist didn't call him on it, Matt lost interest in the session. We finally found a doctor who Matt trusted, but, in a cruel twist of fate, the doctor died a month later in a car accident in London.

Matt was truly never the same after that rape, and neither were Dennis and I. We constantly worried about his physical safety and his mental state. We worried that he might never feel safe, and we worried that the despair might, someday, lead him to hurt himself.

MATT'S HIGH SCHOOL GRADUATION, in the spring of 1995, didn't end our geographical separation. In fact, it took him thousands of miles farther away, to Salisbury, North Carolina, where he enrolled at Catawba College—a private, liberal arts college with about one thousand students. I'd never been to North Carolina and had never heard of Catawba, but I was encouraged by the reasoning behind Matt's decision to go there: Catawba wasn't only the alma mater of one of his favorite teachers in Switzerland—his English teacher, his adviser, and his friend—but it was also consistently ranked among the top ten theater colleges in the country. His selection of the school, and his plan to sign up for theater classes there, seemed like a strong signal that Matt was finally on the mend. Granted, it was a small sign, but it was enough for

Dennis and me to give the college our wholehearted stamp of approval.

Another indication that our son was doing better came in the form of one of the first middle-of-the-night phone calls he made upon moving to Salisbury. I hadn't yet grown accustomed to Matt's disregard for time zones, or his enduring indifference to the fact that 7:00 p.m. in North Carolina meant 3:00 a.m. in Saudi Arabia, so the ringing telephone didn't just shake me awake, it set my heart racing.

"Hello?" I coughed, as anxiousness seemed to strangle my throat.

"Mom?" he answered, in a whisper that did nothing to calm my nerves.

"Matt? What is it? What time is it?"

"Mom, I need to tell you something," he said.

"What do you need to tell me?"

"I need to tell you that I'm gay."

I think it probably took me a couple seconds to say anything back, and I'm sure that for him those were the longest seconds in the world. He'd just opened his heart and told me what I imagine was probably his deepest secret at the time. Aside from complete rejection, the last thing he wanted was silence. But as long as I had anticipated this moment, I hadn't rehearsed anything to say when it finally came. And I didn't want to say just anything—I had to say the right thing.

"What took you so long to tell me?" I finally asked, before explaining that I'd always known and had just been waiting for him to figure it out for himself.

If it were possible to hear stress release from a person's body, I could hear it fall off Matt's back and shoulders that night. "How did you know before I did?" he asked, surprised and at the same time playful.

"It's just a mom thing. I don't think you can keep something like that from the person who knows you best."

We continued back and forth like that for about twenty minutes before the discussion turned somewhat serious; he wasn't yet ready for "everyone" to know. By "everyone," he meant his father. Matt worried about how Dennis might react, and while I could understand that his fear was real, I told him that he had nothing to worry about. No one loved Matt more than his father and I did, and there was nothing that could ever change that. Still, I told Matt that I'd keep his secret until he was ready to tell his dad.

I'm pretty good at keeping my word, but in the thirty-six years that Dennis and I have been married there's little or nothing I've kept from him. So as soon as Dennis got home, I told him what Matt had just told me.

While I'd always suspected that Matt might be gay, the thought had never crossed Dennis's mind. Even though he wasn't upset at the prospect of having a gay son, he didn't think Matt knew what he was talking about. "He just hasn't found the right girl yet," he said, in what I now know is a fairly ordinary—if misguided—parental response.

"I can understand how you might think that," I said. "And you might be right that he hasn't found the right person yet. But you're going to have to get used to the fact that that person is going to be a man, not a woman."

"Okay, I get it," he eventually said. "It might take me a while to get used to it, but I get it."

That was pretty much the extent of our discussion about Matt coming out. Of course, we had many other conversations that revolved around sexual orientation—and many that included Matt—but there was never any more talk about whether Matt really was gay or whether he should be gay. He was simply our son, and we loved him.

The only difficult part of having Dennis know that Matt had come out of the closet was that we couldn't let Matt know that I'd told him. So Dennis and Matt weren't able to talk about it for a couple of years.

That didn't keep Matt from talking with me, though. Part of the reason he decided to tell me in the first place was that he'd started dating someone in North Carolina and wanted to share it with me. Thinking about Matt dating made me think of him being intimate with another person. I'd told both Matt and his brother that I didn't really want to know anything about any of their sexual encounters. I assumed, once they were a certain age, they might be engaging in sex. I also hoped, based on many conversations that Dennis and I had with the boys, that they would be careful and cautious when they decided to become sexually active. But, just as most kids don't want to know the details of their parents having sex, I didn't want to know any of the details of either of my sons' sexual activities. Today I realize that this is one of the bigger roadblocks when it comes to people accepting gay people—particularly gay men. Some folks think being gay is only about having sex with someone of the same gender, and that's the last thing many people want to think about. Now that I've become friends with so many gay people, my eyes have opened to the fact that, straight or gay, sexual orientation is about so much more than just who you go to bed with. It's about relationships. Relationships that are like any other. It can be joyous and sad and sometimes unsuccessful. But like so many other people, it took me a while to figure that out.

Therefore Matt and I didn't really talk about the guy he dated while he was in North Carolina. I found out later that it was a relationship with a lot of ups and downs, breakups and making up and broken hearts. I'm sure it didn't help that Matt was dealing with a series of less-than-ideal roommates at the time. He said that the first, a Gulf War veteran who was six years older than him, was homophobic and constantly hurling slurs and beer cans at him. Then, after the school took care of that situation, Matt was paired up with a perfectly nice guy who grew marijuana in their dorm room. The combined stress was too much for his already fragile mental state. By spring semester, even though he finally had a good roommate, he stopped attending classes, fell into an undiagnosed depression, and made the first of several moves. He told Dennis and me that he thought everything would clear up if he could just go somewhere else, find a change of scenery, and make new friends. His first move was 150 miles east, to Raleigh, where he found a job at a video store and started to see a new therapist. I remember that Matt was particularly excited about this doctor, partly because the psychiatrist was, I believe, one of the few in the country who was using a pioneering new blink therapy to combat post-traumatic stress disorder. Matt had read about the treatment in a magazine or newspaper article and thought it might finally be the key to his recovery.

But recovery wasn't the only thing on his mind. Like most nineteen-year-olds living by themselves in a large city for the first time, Matt also set out to have a good time once he got to Raleigh. He became a regular at the gay bars in town, became friends with a number of the patrons, and adopted what I guess could be called a bit of a club-kid persona, wearing makeup and incorporating flashier clothes into his wardrobe. Under normal circumstances, this wouldn't have bothered me. I, as much as anybody, understand the need—especially at that age—to get out on your own, spread your wings, and learn a little bit from your decisions, good or bad. But these weren't normal circumstances. Matt was taking prescription drugs, and the alcohol that came part and parcel with the bar scene not only messed with the efficacy of the medication but also strengthened his depression. Little distractions were amplified in his mind. And larger disturbances—like Hurricane Fran, which was the worst hurricane to hit North Carolina in a half century—scared him half to death.

Matt also told me that he was troubled by the prejudice he witnessed in North Carolina. He'd never really lived anywhere that was as racially diverse as the South, so he'd never really had to deal with racism. It made him sick when he came face-to-face with it. He had witnessed a Ku Klux Klan rally when he was living in Salisbury. He stayed in Raleigh for about six months before he decided that another move was in order—this time back home to Casper.

CHAPTER

Six

MATT'S DECISION TO MOVE BACK to Wyoming coincided with my own return home. Logan was leaving Saudi Arabia that fall to attend boarding school in Minnesota, so I decided to go back to Wyoming to pursue a master's degree in Elizabethan history and U.S. constitutional law at Casper College. I think Matt was as thrilled as I was at the idea of us living together in the same city again, especially because we weren't actually going to be living together. Dennis and I had sold our family home when we moved to Saudi Arabia, so Matt and I both had to find a new place to live. We decided to get separate apartments in the same complex. That way he'd have the freedom he desired, and I'd have the peace and quiet I'd need to study.

I was especially looking forward to being together with Matt in Casper because I felt the special bond that we'd always shared when he was growing up—the one that formed out of necessity when Dennis was on the road and Matt and I were the only ones at home—had become strained since we'd left the state. I'd assumed that part of that strain was just the result of him being a teenager and feeling that he'd grown out of the need for doting parents. But I also thought a good deal of it had to do with distance and the difficulty it posed when it came to staying in touch.

In many ways, living in the same apartment complex as Matt was just as I hoped it would be. We spent as much time together as we could, picking up right where we'd left off, with dinners, movie nights, and hour-long conversations about the news of the day. But most of our days were spent apart—mine in the classroom and Matt's revolving around his new network of friends.

Today, remembering the short time that Matt and I lived together in that Casper apartment complex, I have to fight the instinct to second-guess myself. Why didn't I spend more time with him? Why, when I knew that he was still having trouble with flashbacks and blackouts related to the rape in Morocco, didn't I insist that he find a local therapist he could trust? But then I have to remind myself that all my thoughts about Matt back then were based on the basic theory that he needed to learn to work through these problems on his own, without nagging from his father and me. I also assumed that Matt would have plenty of time to figure it out and that I'd always get to spend time with him later, when we were both less busy.

So when, six months after we'd moved back to Casper, Matt announced that he wanted to follow one of his new openly gay friends, Romaine Patterson, to Denver, I didn't quibble. Just as with the moves to Raleigh and to Casper, Matt thought this move would solve his problems. Going back to the big city, he reasoned, would make him happy again. And, wrapped up as I was in my textbooks, I didn't question his thinking. I hoped, as much as I assume he did, that a move to Denver really was the answer, or at least the beginning of the answer, to all of his problems. But I definitely didn't spend as much time analyzing the pros and cons as I would have if presented with the same proposition today.

Things actually did start to look up for Matt in Denver. Sure, his one-bedroom downtown apartment left a bit to be desired. Evidently the bars on the windows were there for good reason; almost weekly Matt reported that the police were surrounding his block for what seemed like drug busts. Still, he did what he could with the place—hanging art posters to brighten up the rooms and displaying a collection of small glass bottles to make the place feel more like his own.

He secured a job right away, working at a customer-service telephone bank sort of thing, where he answered people's questions about various vitamins. He didn't like it at all, but it paid the rent. Matt said that he felt like he was lying because he had to pretend like he was an expert when he really just sat there with a tabbed three-ring binder and read back what his bosses told him to say. His plan was to stick around until he gained residency in Colorado and could get in-state tuition and go back to college.

When he wasn't at work, he spent a good deal of the day hanging out at Diedrich Coffee, where Romaine worked, drinking coffee, smoking cigarettes, and bending the ear of anyone willing to listen. Romaine later told me that Matt's favorite drink was a skim-milk latte, which he'd nurse for hours before asking Romaine or someone else behind the counter to reheat it—with a steam wand rather than a microwave, because it tasted better that way.

I was thankful for Matt's friendship with Romaine. Although she'd grown up in Wyoming, she'd spent a lot of time as a teenager in Denver with her three older gay brothers. Her familiarity with the city made me more comfortable about Matt being there.

With all the new things in his life, he couldn't seem to shake his depression. He was still being treated with antidepression and antianxiety drugs, but he wasn't taking them as prescribed. He'd forget to take them on the good days and take too many of them on the bad days, and he continued to drink.

By this time, I'd returned to Saudi Arabia. I probably should have been concerned when Matt's calls home were mostly complaints. The same thing had happened when he started to have trouble in North Carolina. He was the kind of kid who'd forget to call when things were going great, but if things were not so great, he would call. When Matt did start calling, he was complaining about how difficult it was to get around the city and how he wished Dennis and I would get one of the family cars out of storage for him. (There was no way we were going to do that, though. Matt was a horrible driver, and the last thing we wanted to do was to put him behind the wheel in Denver.) Next he started to tell us how he hated his job. The real red flag, though, should have been when Matt didn't make it to Saudi Arabia for Christmas. Just as for all his trips in and out of Saudi Arabia, Matt was required to fill out paperwork for a visitor visa before he could come. But he put off the paperwork until it was too late. He later told me that he spent all Christmas day in bed, with the covers up over his head. What I didn't know at the time was that the signs of clinical depression include an inability to control negative thoughts, difficulty concentrating on and completing tasks at hand, and a withdrawal from social functions.

It was nearly a month later, in January 1998, that we finally got an inkling of just how badly things had spiraled out of control for Matt. It had been a couple of weeks since we'd heard much from him; then we got a call from Dennis's sister-in-law saying that Matt had called her house to tell her that he was in trouble and frightened. He asked if she could come get him.

When she reached the apartment, Matt's aunt found that her nephew truly was in trouble. He clearly hadn't been bathing or eating and hadn't left his apartment for days. The place was a mess, his clothes were filthy, and there was a stench that she remembered as smelling like rotten food. I was really baffled when Matt later told me that he had first sought help from St. John's Episcopal Cathedral, across the street from his apartment, and was told that there wasn't anything they could do to assist him, and then told that he needed to leave. I had always thought churches were, first and foremost, there to help those in trouble. I guess that isn't always the case.

Dennis's sister-in-law immediately took Matt to the hospital, where doctors diagnosed his depression, realized that he'd been self-medicating, and prescribed yet another round of drugs.

Living half a world away in Saudi Arabia, it was difficult for Dennis and me to know exactly what was or wasn't going on in Matt's life. But it didn't seem to either one of us that a new prescription would be the answer, especially since Matt already had so much difficulty sticking to the regimens of prescriptions given to him by all of his previous doctors. However, we were at a loss for what a better solution might be, so when Matt suggested yet another move in the spring of 1998—this time to Laramie—we wholeheartedly endorsed his plan. After everything he'd been through, Matt thought the answer was to go back home and finally get serious about school and get healthy. In May he moved himself to an apartment on Twelfth Street—just a couple blocks from campus—and enrolled in summer school classes at the University of Wyoming. A couple of weeks later, I flew back to Laramie and helped Matt set up his apartment. Since Matt was so frustrated by not having his own transportation in Denver, I also got the '78 Bronco out of storage so he could use it in Laramie. I remember thinking at the time that things were finally starting to look up for my son.

CHAPTER

Seven

IN AUGUST 1998—three months after Matt had moved to Laramie—Dennis, Logan, Matt, and I all met in Casper for vacation. It had been five years since we first moved to Saudi Arabia, five years since Matt first left home for boarding school in Switzerland, and two years since Logan, who was now seventeen, started high school in Minnesota. We'd all been back to Wyoming—together and separately—during those five years, but this trip was different. Dennis and I were looking forward to it more than any of the others because, in addition to being a rare opportunity to spend four weeks with the boys, it was a chance for us to really check in with Matt. His depression—the anxiety attacks, the medications, and his difficulties finding a doctor—was always on our minds. Matt's inability to get better had made him frustrated and angry over the past couple of years, and we knew that he had high hopes for this move to Wyoming. The vacation was going to be our chance to observe him and to reassure ourselves that our son was finally on the right track.

The plan was for the four of us to meet in Casper before driving across the state to Yellowstone National Park—for our first visit there as a family. We would then drive to the Bighorn Mountains east of the park, to camp and fish with Dennis's folks. At first everything went off as planned. After a night in Casper, we packed up our '91 Honda Accord and headed out on the six-hour journey to Yellowstone's east entrance. When we arrived in Cody, Wyoming, about forty miles from the park gates, we checked into the Holiday Inn. I had an aunt living in town, so we took her to dinner that night and had a nice evening of reminiscing. After dinner we returned to our rooms, Logan and Matt in one, and Dennis and me in another. I told the boys to get to bed so we could hit the road early and beat the crowd into the park. Like any first-time visitors, the boys were excited about seeing Old Faithful and, of course, hoping that we'd run into a few moose or perhaps even a grizzly bear.

But when we called the boys' room the next morning, Logan answered and said, "Matt's not here; he's at the police station."

"He's what?" I asked, not fully able to comprehend what Logan was telling me. We weren't in the middle of nowhere, but Cody was a town of only about eight thousand people. How in the heck could Matt get in trouble here? And weren't he and Logan just going to sleep a few hours ago?

It turned out that as Logan was getting ready to go to bed,

Matt, true to his restless nature, snuck out of the hotel and de-manded that his brother not say anything. He promised Logan that he'd be back before it was time to leave for Yellowstone. "No one will even know I'm gone," he reassured his brother.

After leaving the hotel, Matt made his way to a popular bar in the center of town. He sidled up to the bar, where he or-dered a couple of beers and, in the process, befriended the bar-tender. After the bar closed at 1:30 a.m., the bartender asked if Matt wanted to join him and a few friends on a drive up to Newton Lakes, just north of town, to watch the stars. Matt, who never missed an opportunity to pass the time with friends, new or old, accepted the invitation.

The group continued drinking when they got to the lake. As Matt later told me, a couple of the people he was with—a young man and woman—started making out with each other. Hoping to give the couple a little privacy, he said he asked the bartender if he wanted to go for a walk. But the bartender turned him down. When Matt persisted, grabbing him by the shirt and asking him to leave the lovers alone, the bartender punched Matt twice in the jaw, knocking him unconscious for a couple of minutes with the second punch.

The bartender, who was straight, later said that he thought Matt was making a pass at him—that Matt wasn't concerned about the others' privacy but was trying to coax him behind the truck for some intimacy of their own. He only punched Matt as a last resort, he said, after my son wouldn't take no for an answer. I question the bartender's interpretation of Matt's behavior. Matt told me several times—before and after the incident in Cody—that he'd never flirt with a straight guy. "It's pointless," he said. "It's a waste of time. A waste of energy." Thinking about it today, I suppose it's possible that both Matt and the bartender were telling the truth. Matt really was thinking of the other couple's privacy when he suggested the walk, and the bartender—perhaps a little paranoid that he was with an openly gay guy, albeit one who was barely more than five feet tall—freaked out about what he thought was a come-on and felt that he needed to punch Matt out in order to assert his manhood.

Whatever the reasons behind the altercation, it broke up the make-out session, as one might expect, and triggered something dangerous in Matt—what appeared to be a flashback to the rape he suffered in Morocco. So after the group left the lake and drove Matt back to the hotel, he started causing a commotion, telling people that he'd been raped and demanding that the front-desk clerk call the police.

Dennis and I slept through the ruckus, and Logan, who was understandably freaked out by everything he witnessed after Matt was ushered back to their hotel room, honored his brother's request to keep quiet. After the police arrived and took Matt to the station, he told them that he thought he'd been raped out by the lake. But after tests at the local hospital showed no signs of sexual assault (and the only sign of any altercation was a bloody lip), Matt decided against filing charges, saying he'd had too much to drink to remember any of the actual details.

We were furious when we found out what happened. After everything settled down, I demanded, "Why couldn't you have just spent the night in the hotel with the rest of us? Why did you feel the need to go out?" We were angry, but a little dumbfounded, too. At this point we hadn't lived with Matt for a good while, and though we knew he was restless, we hadn't realized how easily that feeling manifested itself into recklessness.

Matt was horribly embarrassed by what had happened, and I think he was mortified that Dennis, Logan, and I witnessed it all. He told us that the bartender's punch immediately sent him back to that night in Morocco, which made him black out of reality and think he was being raped once again.

We, of course, understood that he was still suffering from the aftereffects of the attack three years before. But by this point, we didn't buy it as an adequate excuse for his behavior that night. His decisions since the rape—including his blatant disregard for the schedule prescribed with the drugs doctors had been giving him to help with his anxiety and depression—were also to blame. Matt only remembered to take the drugs when he wasn't feeling well, so the pills only seemed to help with the troubles at hand, rather than the bigger picture. And because the pills weren't working in the way he wanted—because he wasn't taking them in the way he was supposed to—he'd often follow them up with several glasses of wine or a couple of bottles of beer. And as anybody who knows anything about alcohol and prescription drugs realizes, Matt was more than just hindering his chances of recovery: He was spiraling out of control.

Dennis and I'd already had stern words with him about this several times, but the incident in Cody made it clear that our warnings hadn't gotten through. We tried to talk with him again. We especially warned him about alcohol abuse. We tried to not take a holier-than-thou stand—Dennis and I met at a fraternity party after all. But there was something different about the way kids drank when we were in college and the way Matt was drinking now. Where we'd have a few drinks and then stop, he'd just keep going—often until he blacked out. We'd warned him about alcohol abuse since he was in junior high, and we did so again in Cody. Matt was ashamed by what he'd put his family through, and swore that he'd do better—and get better—now that he was back in school in Laramie.

I'm not sure that Dennis and I believed Matt as much as we tried to take him at his word. It always seemed like there was something standing in the way of his recuperation. While we were sure that he wasn't to blame for all the roadblocks, everything we'd witnessed in Cody suggested that, whether he knew it or not, Matt sometimes stood in his own way. And as long as his friends and family continued to enable him by doing his laundry and grocery shopping when he didn't feel like getting out of bed, or patting him on the head and saying, "Everything will be okay, honey"—Matt was probably never going to get any better. We thought he would have to learn to do things for himself.

Looking back, the Cody incident must have been a tipping point for us as parents, pushing us into what you could call the tough-love portion of Matt's growing up. We desperately wanted to take his hand and lead him to the right doctors, call him a half hour before every appointment to make sure he'd make it on time, and convince him of the need to take his drugs as prescribed (meaning every day and without alcohol). But we'd tried that. By now it was painfully clear that hadn't worked. Matt was nearly twenty-two, and it was time he took responsibility for his actions. If that meant that Dennis and I needed to let go and let Matt fend for himself, so be it. Matt needed to make life work on his own terms, rather than let other people—longtime friends or a bartender he'd just met—dictate his life for him.

So even though we were in despair that day in Cody (really, what parents wouldn't be?), we did our best not to make a bigger deal of what happened than Matt already had. We didn't hover over him, we didn't condemn him, and we didn't do much to try to make him feel better. We told him that he knew better than to put himself in a position like that, and we agreed when Matt said that it was high time he got his life in order. Then Dennis and I pretty much let things be. In retrospect, I'm not sure if that was the right tactic, but at the time it was what we thought best.

THERE WAS NO AVOIDING the subject of Matt's sexual orientation after we picked him up from the Cody police station that morning, though. It was sort of the elephant in the room when one of our first questions for him was, "Why would the bartender think you were trying to hook up with him?" So the time to tell his dad had finally arrived. However, I think the situation made it even more difficult for Matt to tell the truth, so he told his dad that the bartender had only guessed Matt was gay.

Obviously we didn't make it to Yellowstone that day as planned, and as a result of Matt's incident, we were late meeting Dennis's folks at the campground. We spent the rest of the week as we'd expected to—fishing, camping, playing cards, just visiting. Whatever we did seemed to be overshadowed by what had happened in Cody. We couldn't seem to shake the shock and disappointment that we were still feeling. Although we didn't tell Dennis's parents what had happened, instead explaining the swollen lip by saying Matt had been in a bit of a scuffle, the rest of us knew. Unfortunately, those feelings really cast a pall over what the four of us had hoped would be the perfect time together. At the end of the camping trip, Matt hugged both his grandparents and made plans to see them in Laramie.

If one good thing came out of what happened in Cody, it's

that the following week, when we were all in Minnesota, Matt finally told Dennis that he was gay. The four of us had flown to Minnesota to celebrate my father's nintieth birthday. He and my mother were now living in an assisted-living facility in Minneapolis near my sister. While there we planned to take Logan back to his high school, which was located thirty-five miles south of the city.

I'm not sure what part of that situation made Matt think it was time to tell his dad, but something was different. Of course, Dennis already knew and had only been waiting for Matt to tell him. With every day that Matt kept his dad out of the loop, I saw the anxiety build around whatever scary scenario he'd created in his head about telling Dennis who he was. When he did find the opportunity to tell his dad, the lack of a shocked or surprised response made Matt think that Dennis didn't care, which couldn't be further from the truth. He cared a great deal. It's just that he'd already known about Matt's sexual orientation for several years, and he was trying to balance what should have been an element of surprise with a response that he hoped would convey acceptance. He wanted to show that the news wouldn't change a thing between the two of them. He made it clear that it didn't matter that Matt was gay. He told him he would always be his son and that he would always love him. To be fair to Dennis, even if he hadn't already known that Matt was gay, the revelation paled in comparison to everything the family had been through in the previous day or two.

Buoyed by what he saw as a positive experience coming out to his father, Matt hinted that he wanted to come out to more of the family when we were in Minnesota. I know he told my mother while visiting with her and my father at their apartment. She told me later she didn't see what all the fuss was about. "If you're gay, you're gay." I asked her if Matt could introduce her to some of his friends but she refused. She said, "I love Matt. He's my grandson. That doesn't mean I will like his friends." It was a start anyway. I think he also came out to his cousin on that trip. However, the only lasting memory I have of our time there is of a family barbecue where Matt ended up drinking too much wine, making a fool of himself, and further underscoring our concern for him and his state of mind.

This only confirmed our decision to take the tough-love tack. So we didn't speak to Matt about our displeasure and embarrassment when he spilled wine all over himself or when he fell, drunk, in the yard during the barbecue. Dennis and I decided against making any more of a scene or having another overwrought conversation about how he needed to shape up. Our son was a smart enough guy to know that he was screwing up and needed to get better. I was still hopeful that, despite what we'd witnessed during the previous week, Matt was ready to take those first steps to recovery when he got back to Laramie and started school.

After leaving Logan in Minnesota, Dennis and I returned to Laramie with Matt before heading back to Saudi Arabia.

There was nothing particularly remarkable about that visit—other than that we told Matt how proud we were of him and how hopeful we were for his first semester at the University of Wyoming. Matt had struggled with demons for three years, and when we left him in Laramie, I was very optimistic that he was finally prepared to come out on top.

Although Dennis and I were trying to stick to the tough-love approach on the emotional front, we were still fully supporting Matt financially, which meant paying his tuition at the university and sending him an allowance every month to cover his rent, food, and other expenses. It was enough that Matt could focus on his studies for once and not have to work while he was in school. It wasn't a lot of spending money, maybe a few hundred dollars a month, but enough for him to hang out with friends every once in a while.

At first, Matt didn't know too many people in Laramie. But despite all his other difficulties, he never had trouble making friends—striking up conversations with kids after class or with strangers at the Student Union Building. He also joined the Lesbian, Gay, Bisexual, and Transgendered Alliance (LGBTA) on campus and became friends with a number of other gay (and gay-friendly) people around town.

I didn't realize it at the time, but hanging out with friends was a bit more of a production for Matt than it had been for me when I was in Laramie twenty years before. After living in bigger cities like Raleigh and Denver, he'd grown used to being able to spend his weekend nights socializing at the local gay bars. But there weren't (and still aren't) any gay bars in the whole state of Wyoming. The closest thing was a couple of bars, Nightingales and the Tornado Club, in Fort Collins, Colorado, which is forty miles south of Laramie by way of a winding mountain pass. Matt preferred the Tornado Club, which I understand was the more neighborhood-like of the two, and often tried to hitch rides down there with friends on Friday nights.

I still shudder when I think of those eighty-mile round-trips to the bars in Fort Collins—especially the late-night drive home. And I'm relieved that Matt never wanted to make the drive himself. The Bronco that we left with him was very reliable, but it was huge and pretty difficult to maneuver. So Matt, who never had much faith in his own driving skills, only got behind the wheel when he absolutely needed to or for a quick trip across town. As foolhardy as Matt was sometimes, he was very careful to not drink and drive or to be in a car with a drunk driver, for that matter.

Matt was pretty resourceful though. He never let the lack of a ride keep him from going to Fort Collins. I didn't know this at the time, but I found out later that when he couldn't find a friend who was willing to be a designated driver, he'd shell out a hundred dollars or more to hire a chauffeured limousine to drive him back and forth to the gay bar.

If that sounds extravagant and a little bit beyond Matt's

means, you're right. The allowance we gave him every month was nowhere near enough to pay for chauffeured limousines, and it soon became clear that he was using more than his spending money to pay for his social life. Toward the end of September I got a call from Dennis's dad, who was concerned because he got a "phone disconnected" message when he tried to telephone Matt.

After a little bit of digging I learned that Matt wasn't paying his bills. To be fair, he had tried to pay a couple of them, but those checks bounced. It seems a little silly to say it today, but I flipped out at the news. Maybe there was some residual anger left over from what had happened in Cody, but I was suddenly at my wit's end. My first concern was practical: If his home phone wasn't working, that meant he was using his cell phone—which cost more than twice as much as the landline—to make calls. Then I was consumed by the bigger picture. What more did Dennis and I have to do in order for Matt to accept some responsibility? From what I could tell, we were giving him all the tools he needed to put his life in order, but what hope did we have for that actually happening if he couldn't even make sure his phone didn't get disconnected?

So I called Matt on his cell phone, which was still working, to let him have it. It was a Saturday morning after he'd just returned from one of his trips to Fort Collins. I'm sure the last thing he wanted to do was talk to me about responsibility, phone bills, and checking-account balances. But I didn't know what he'd been up to the night before, nor did I care. It was time to talk some sense into him. And he had no sooner said hello than I laid into him. "Matt, explain this to me," I demanded. "Your dad and I are giving you the money to pay the bills, but your bank account is empty and the bills aren't being paid. What's going on? What are you spending the money on?" He had some harsh words for me in return: "You're being too controlling," "Leave me alone," and that sort of thing. Then he cussed me out a little bit, which wasn't like him. We went back and forth like that for a few minutes, accomplishing absolutely nothing, until Matt hung up on me.

I didn't call him back. As close as we'd always been, we'd fought like that before. Matt had always been hot tempered— even before he started suffering from depression—and his fury was usually aimed at Dennis, Logan, or me. While Dennis and I understood that Matt's anger was somehow tied to some frustration he probably felt in relation to his need to come to terms with his sexual orientation, Logan was mystified by his brother's tantrums. Years later Logan told me that he just assumed his brother was a jerk some of the time. But Matt's manic reactions made much more sense to Logan after Matt had come out to him. He better understood everything his brother had been going through on a personal level for most of his life. I had hoped that now that we all knew who Matt was and, more important, could discuss it with him and among one another, these outbursts would be fewer and farther between.

As upset as Matt would get, he never stayed angry for long. True to form, he called me on Monday, October 5, and apologized—for cursing at me, for not paying his phone bill, and for being so haphazard with his allowance. We only talked for a few minutes—after his apology, most of our conversation was small talk. He was excited about his classes (especially his political science class), he felt like he was getting a cold, and he planned on attending an LGBTA meeting the following day to help plan activities for National Coming Out Day on October 11. I told him that his dad had been busy with work, but that I'd been keeping myself occupied with the usual stuff and that I loved him. He said again that he was sorry for everything and he loved me too. Then we hung up.

I thought about that last phone conversation again three days later, as Dennis and I were flying across the Atlantic to Matt's side at the hospital in Fort Collins. My son and I had said so little to each other on Monday. It was the kind of conversation you share with the people you love because you assume that you'll have a chance to catch up again in a matter of days. But I was suddenly so grateful for that short call. If what the doctor in Laramie had told us was true—that the damage to Matt's brain stem was so severe that, if he were to live, he'd likely never wake up—then it was clear that he and I would never have another conversation. I couldn't shake the thought that if Matt hadn't taken the time to call me and apologize on Monday, the argument we'd had on Saturday (as silly and as trivial as it ultimately was) would have been our last conversation.

Our time together a month and a half before had been difficult for all of us, and as frustrated and perplexed as Dennis, Logan, and I had been by Matt's activity in Cody, we'd all had a chance to put our relationship with him on good terms. I was so very, very thankful for that—and still am.

Eight

On Friday, October 9, 1998, twenty hours after Dennis and I left Saudi Arabia, we landed at the St. Paul/Minneapolis airport—to pick up Logan and fly on to Denver. We hadn't said much to Logan when we called from Saudi Arabia, just that Matt had been hurt, we were coming to pick him up, and that he needed to be sure to pack some nice clothes. We were vague with Logan partly because we didn't know much. The most we'd heard was from the doctor at the hospital in Laramie, which wasn't adequately equipped to identify the full extent of his injuries. So not only did we not know how Matt had been hurt, or who had attacked him, we didn't know for certain how severely he'd been hurt.

But we would have been nonspecific in that first conversation with Logan even if we did have more details. It would be a full day before we'd be able to meet Logan in Minneapolis. I didn't want my younger son to have to deal with the weight of the details on his own.

My sister, Kay, her daughter Kristen, and Logan were at the gate when we landed. (Obviously, this was in the days before airport security prevented anyone without a boarding pass to be in the gate area.) I could immediately tell by looking at Kay that she knew more about Matt than I did, and that it wasn't good news. There wasn't one thing about her expression that gave it away but a combination of the way her eyes met mine, in a pleading and sorrowful way, and the lack of color in her face when I came off the Jetway. Logan, on the other hand, was almost jovial to see Dennis and me, so I was sure he knew nothing more than what we'd told him on the phone.

I think I can best describe what I imagine it was like for Logan by comparing it to most people's experience when they first heard that two planes had crashed into the World Trade Center on the morning of September 11. Unless we saw the terrorist acts live on TV, most of us assumed that the aircraft were small single-engine or prop planes, that the collisions were a result of pilot error. Until we saw what had happened with our own eyes—and in many cases, not for hours or days afterward—we couldn't understand the gravity of what had really happened because we had no experience with which to compare it.

After we called Logan I think he probably assumed that Matt had been in another dustup like the one in Cody. Maybe a split lip and a broken nose were the worst situations that we'd have to deal with.

We had expected that speaking to Logan was going to be

difficult. In anticipation of that, Dennis and I talked about strategies during the flight to Minneapolis for softening the blow. We ultimately decided to simply take it as it came, to follow Logan's reactions, and to be as honest as we could. When it came time to sit him down in the airport, and tell him what little we did know about what had happened to Matt, it felt more mechanical than emotional. Dennis took him aside and told him what we knew. It was just another thing we needed to get through. The news shocked him, just as it had his father and me, but Logan didn't cry out or ask a lot of questions. He just sat there quietly, stared at us, and listened.

At that point I never imagined Logan would be the last person to whom I would have to break the news about Matt. It wasn't until after Logan, Dennis, and I spoke and started to move to our next gate that I began to understand the look in Kay's eyes. I began to suspect that Matt's condition was worse than we thought and that it was now more than a family matter.

I walked past a newsstand and, out of the corner of my eye, saw that there was a story about Matt in at least two newspapers—the *New York Times* and the *Minneapolis Star Tribune*. I only remember one of the headlines: "Gay Man Beaten and Left for Dead; 2 Are Charged." Granted, nothing really made sense to me at that point, but the headline was truly confusing. It was as if I were living out a scene in a movie or novel. Of course my family was incredibly worried about Matt, but I couldn't imagine why his attack would be newsworthy in Minnesota, much less New York City. The only reason I could fathom that the story would be of any concern outside of Wyoming was if the press was reporting that the attack had to do with Matt's sexual orientation. The headline suggested that they were.

Until then the only gay-related news I'd ever seen or read had been exploitive *National Enquirer*–type stuff. So when I saw those headlines in Minneapolis, my imagination and worst fears made me shudder; if the papers were reporting that Matt was gay, they were probably saying that he was attacked because he was gay, and that being beaten was his own fault.

Despite the fact that I hadn't really heard any news about Matt, my first reaction wasn't to pick up the papers and read the articles about him. Instead I just started to cry. Kay took my arm and whispered, "You can't let Logan see you like this." Knowing she was right, I regained my composure. I tried to buy one of the newspapers anyway, before Dennis grabbed me by the other shoulder and said, "I don't know if we really want to read that." We didn't discuss it any further, but I knew he was right. There was so much occupying our minds that there was absolutely no room for false information. If we didn't have the full story, the newspapers couldn't have it either. As far as I knew, their columns were filled with a lot of speculation and misinformation. Once I stopped to think about that, I realized that I didn't want to know anything about Matt until I could get to Fort Collins and find out the real story for myself.

*　　*　　*

DENNIS, LOGAN, AND I flew to Denver in near silence, without any discussion of what we'd find when we arrived in Fort Collins. But when we landed, we couldn't avoid the story that the attack had become. As our plane pulled up to its gate, a flight attendant gave us a note asking us to remain on the plane. Then, once the other passengers left, it was explained to us that, because of the possibility of press waiting for us at the gate, Denver police officers would meet us outside on the jet bridge and drive us to the main terminal to pick up our luggage.

It was another level in the descent to my suddenly surreal existence. I remember just sitting there with the note, looking at Dennis, and thinking, "What in the heck are they talking about? Press at the gate? Who do they think we are? Elton John or something?" To me, everybody seemed to be overreacting. Whether it was because I didn't understand the scope of what was happening or didn't want to comprehend it, I suddenly got very possessive. This was about our son. This was about our family. And I didn't want any other people around— no matter how admirable or helpful their intentions were.

As it turned out, I don't think there was any press at the gate. In fact, it probably would have been pointless for reporters to be there since nobody knew what we looked like yet. Still, as soon as we arrived at the baggage claim I could tell that I was going to lose it again. So, still thinking of Logan, I immediately excused myself and ran into the ladies' room. It wasn't until I got there—in the bathroom and away from my son, my husband, and the mob of reporters who would trail us for the next few weeks—that the full weight of the situation hit.

Everything I'd done in my life since marrying Dennis was with my family foremost in mind. Now, for the first time, it seemed like there was nothing I could do to protect anybody, including myself. Even worse, our tragedy was about to unfold under the scrutiny of TV cameras and reporters' notebooks. The feeling of helplessness morphed into a wave of nausea that forced me to rush to a stall and throw up.

Once we exited the terminal, my brother, Jim, and Dennis's brother, Steve, and his family, were there waiting for us to take us to the hospital in Fort Collins.

The hospital had given Steve instructions on how to get us there in the quietest way possible. We were to park in a convenience store parking lot and call the hospital. They would then send someone from hospital security to take us to a certain door to avoid the press waiting in the front lobby. We thought that was a little dramatic because we were unaware of what was happening at the hospital. Security had been placed at every entrance to the neurosurgical intensive care unit (ICU), where Matt's room was located. People who had no reason to be there, other than to try and get information about Matt, were attempting to bypass security. It was chaos. Reporters were everywhere, as well as both well-wishers and those who wished Matt harm.

Nine

WHEN PEOPLE ASK ME what it was like to see Matt in the hospital for the first time, I sometimes think that they're less interested (on a subconscious level at least) in hearing my experiences than they are in getting my assurance that they'd be able to handle a similar situation. Generally, people want to hear that they wouldn't scream, that their knees wouldn't buckle, or that they'd simply be able to keep their self-control. I'm not bothered by their questions; quite the opposite. I more than understand the desire for that kind of peace of mind. But I can't make that promise. I wanted to bawl and fall to my knees when the doctors finally briefed us on the full extent of Matt's condition.

He was in a coma as a result of severe injuries to his skull and brain stem. He couldn't breathe without a ventilator, and his temperature was severely fluctuating between 98 and 106 degrees. There was also the possibility that Matt might be able to pick up on our energy, that our despair might hinder any potential recovery, so Dennis and I took a moment to collect ourselves and to convince each other that we would remain as calm and positive as possible before entering Matt's room.

What we found in the neurological ICU that day was a motionless, unconscious young man, his head swathed in bandages, and tubes everywhere, enabling his body to hold on to life. We heard the machines helping him breathe. We saw the screens monitoring his vital signs. His face was swollen and covered in stitches, and his ear had been stitched and was still bleeding. We couldn't tell if it really was Matt. This young man bore absolutely no resemblance to the split-lipped twenty-one-year-old we'd left in Laramie only a few weeks before.

But as we approached the bed, Dennis and I saw that this was indeed our precious son. We could tell by the cute little bump on the top of his left ear. One of his eyes was partially open, too, and we could see its clear blue color. And who could mistake those long black lashes? The braces, which we could see because his teeth held the tube in his mouth, were unmistakably Matt's. It was clear to both of us that the twinkle of life—his stubborn, restless, curious, and always spontaneous nature—wasn't there.

We stayed in his room for a while—although I don't remember exactly how long—before talking more with a doctor. We did everything we could to let Matt know that we were there with him. We talked to him, we stroked his arms and face, and we held his hands and tried to unfold his fingers, which were curled up into a fist. At one point he started to shake and his limbs went rigid. My heart jumped for a minute, and I thought Matt might be responding to us. But the nurse said it was just an involuntary reaction to touching.

Eventually, we left Matt so we could speak with a doctor and get a full report on his condition. When we did, the news was devastating. Our son had more than thirty bruises, abrasions, and broken bones—including several fractures where his skull had crashed in on itself. As a result, his brain stem, which controlled his heartbeat, breathing, temperature, and other involuntary functions, was severely damaged. He was also suffering from hypothermia. The doctor still didn't know exactly what had caused Matt's injuries. But the damage to the head looked like it was the result of repeated blows with a blunt and heavy object. The first doctor we spoke to in Fort Collins sadly confirmed what we'd heard from the Laramie doctor before leaving Saudi Arabia: It was very unlikely—even close to impossible—that Matt would ever wake up from his coma.

By now Dennis and I were prepared—or as prepared as I suppose we could be—for that likelihood. On the flight over, he and I had talked about the possibility that we'd have to request a do-not-resuscitate order, instructing the hospital not to use "heroic measures" when it was clear that Matt no longer had the strength to live on his own. We'd talked about the issue with the boys before, in one of our countless family discussions; on one occasion it was about my elderly parents. In that talk, Matt made it clear that he never wanted to be on life support. While it was an issue I'd come to terms with regarding my parents, I never thought I would have to consider it for my children.

So when the doctor told us that Matt would likely never wake, we brought up the DNR order and said that our son had expressed a desire to be an organ donor. That's when she told us that, as part of the routine blood work the hospital performed after Matt was admitted, they'd learned that he was HIV positive.

As surprising and as initially devastating as that news would have been a week earlier, on that afternoon it went in one ear and passed out the other. Its only significance, at that moment, was that we wouldn't be able to harvest Matt's organs if and when he died. That was tragic enough in itself, because organ donation was something as important to Matt as it is to Dennis and me.

I've given a lot of thought to Matt's HIV infection since that day, though. At the hospital, the doctor seemed to think Matt's infection was fairly recent because of the relatively high viral load in his blood. HIV and AIDS had been one of my biggest fears ever since I first suspected that Matt might be gay. Back then it seemed as if homosexuality and AIDS went hand in hand. If my hunch was right that Matt was gay, I thought there was a good chance that he'd also end up being HIV positive. Even before he'd come out of the closet, we'd discussed the importance of safe sex. Later, after he'd told me that he was gay, Matt promised me that he'd always use a condom, that he'd never, ever, risk his health. He also told me that he'd been tested for HIV every six months since the rape in Morocco because he was paranoid about seroconversion—and that every little sore throat or sniffle made him worry about it.

I hate to say this, as a mother, but I don't think I would have been a compassionate parent if I'd found out about his HIV status under normal circumstances. I would have been angry and disappointed that Matt hadn't been more careful. I'm not sure I would have been able to resist the urge to say, "Dammit! You promised you would always be careful!" I'm sure I would have been more understanding with time, but my initial reaction may not have been one of compassion.

That Friday evening, in the doctor's office at the hospital in Fort Collins, I had no real feelings about his HIV status, and the only other thought Dennis or I gave to it was to tell family members so that, in case Matt's HIV status came out in the papers, our loved ones wouldn't find out about it there first.

After speaking with that first doctor, a neurosurgeon came in to talk with us more about the injuries to Matt's head, which he confirmed were too severe to expect that our son would ever wake up. He also told us that the damage to Matt's brain had been so severe that he could no longer feel pain. As awful as that information was, it provided me comfort because, with Matt's hands and toes curled up like they were (and as they do for any coma patient), it certainly looked like he was suffering.

To be on the safe side, Dennis and I tried to do everything we could to make Matt as comfortable as possible. We played his favorite CDs (Tracy Chapman and John Fogerty) and sprayed his favorite scents (Jean-Paul Gaultier cologne and a perfume, Anaïs Anaïs, he'd bought me for Christmas). We spoke to him, too. We talked a lot about memories of his years growing up. We also discussed all the things we'd do together when he got out of the hospital. One of the strangest conversations we had was about his hair, which the hospital staff had shaved so they could see all his wounds. It was very uneven. Matt had always been very particular when it came to his hair. "Oh, Matt," I said, "you're not going to like your new haircut!"

We hadn't been there more than a few hours before Dennis decided that he needed to drive to Casper and back—a six-hour round-trip—to get more of Matt's favorite things, including his most treasured childhood stuffed animal, a rabbit named Oscar that the Easter Bunny had given him a long time ago. As important as the stuffed rabbit had been to Matt when he was a kid, we'd never imagined that we'd need it so desperately when we packed up the house before moving to Saudi Arabia. None of the marks we left on any of the boxes in the storage unit directed Dennis to what he was looking for. He tore through box after box—with no luck—before racing back to Fort Collins, where he nearly broke down upon reaching Matt's hospital room.

While Dennis was away in Casper, Rob DeBree of the Albany County Sheriff's Department and Jeff Bury of the Laramie Police Department arrived at the hospital to update me on the evidence that had been gathered in the case. Rob and Jeff, who were both dressed in boots and tweed jackets with pistols at their hips, came by for two reasons. They wanted to tell me about the evidence they were piecing together regarding Matt's attack, and they also needed to ask if I had any information that might help their investigations. They hadn't known Dennis was driving back to Casper.

It surprises me a bit today, when I look back, just how little I knew at that point about the circumstances that had led Matt to being so close to death. I'd still been avoiding both the TV news and the newspapers. The only rumors that had passed my way came from Dennis's sister, who had stayed in the hospital with Matt until we arrived. She told me that she'd heard that Matt had been beaten after being tied to a barbed-wire fence. But when we got to the hospital, it was obvious that his injuries weren't consistent with being tied to a barbed-wire fence—confirming my concern that any information I got before talking to the authorities was going to be wrong, misleading, incomplete, and a waste of time.

If I hadn't lived the nightmare myself, I would have imagined that a mother in the same situation would, from the out-set, do everything she could to find out who'd hurt her son, how they'd done it, and why. It's the sort of story you hear on the cable news networks all the time—the crusading mother out to solve the mystery behind a crime against her child. I suspect that is what people thought Dennis and I were doing as soon as we heard that Matt had been hurt, that we'd been calling the police for constant updates to help piece together the evidence that had been gathered in our son's case. Recog-nizing this, I sometimes have trouble explaining how, at that time, the criminal investigation was the furthest thing from my mind. Even though I knew the truth was probably beyond my most horrible imaginings, I wanted, in the worst way, to know what had happened to Matt—and to understand how in the world something like this could happen to anyone, let alone him. But more than anything else, I still hoped for Matt's recovery. Although it was clear that there was little outside of a miracle that could help our son, Dennis and I didn't want to waste a moment of our precious time thinking about anything but his health and his comfort.

However, I did make an exception when it came to talking to Jeff and Rob for a couple reasons. First I knew that if anyone was going to be able to provide me accurate information re-garding the attack on Matt, it'd be them. Second, even though it wasn't my priority at the time, I knew it was nevertheless my

duty to do whatever I could to help find and prosecute who-
ever was behind this horrendous act.

I don't know if Jeff and Rob were trying to protect me that
first time we met—in a conference area outside Matt's hospital room—but the details they provided came in pretty broad
strokes. Just before Dennis and I received, on that Thursday
morning in Saudi Arabia, the first call from Dr. Cantway at
the Laramie hospital, Matt had been found on the east side of
town, tied to a split-rail fence. News reporters later described
the fence as being far outside town, deep in a Wyoming prairie,
but it was actually within a quarter mile of a housing develop-
ment and not too far from a new Wal-Mart. I think it was the
fence itself that helped stoke this Wyoming prairie mystique.
Although it looked like the kind of fence ranchers historically
used to keep their cattle from roaming, it was just one section
of that kind of fence, placed there to keep trespassers from
driving onto the private property.

Journalists also erroneously reported that Matt had been
"crucified" to the fence, triggering all sorts of questionable
and inappropriate comparisons to Jesus Christ. But Matt was
actually found lying on his side, on the ground, with his hands
tied to the fence rail behind him.

My son was discovered on Wednesday evening (Laramie
time) by Aaron Kreifels, a fellow student at the University of
Wyoming, who saw Matt after he fell nearby during a moun-

tain bike ride. Aaron said that he thought Matt was a Halloween scarecrow at first, a description that might have helped trigger the crucifixion reports. Something led Aaron over to Matt to get a better look. As he got closer, Aaron realized that what he thought was a scarecrow had human hair and he realized he was seeing a person lying on the ground. He ran over to Matt, who he said was unconscious, barely breathing, and caked in blood.

Aaron then ran to the closest home to call the police, and Sheriff's Deputy Reggie Fluty was the first to report to the scene. She said Matt looked so small, crumpled at the foot of the fence, that she first thought he was about thirteen or fourteen years old. The rope tying his hands to the fence was so tight that she had to use a double-bladed boot knife to cut him free. There was blood everywhere—in a pool under his head and all across his face, matted in his hair, and caked around his nostrils—except for tracks on each of his cheeks that had been left by tears. Matt's right eye was open, but his left eye was shut, and she could see a gash above his right ear, which was "caved in and bubbled up on both sides with a film over it where it had bled continuously." As she waited for paramedics to arrive, Reggie said she tried to keep Matt's airway clear of blood while consoling him. "Baby boy, I'm so sorry this happened to you." "What happened to you?" And, "Hang in there, son, help's coming."

Matt was transported to Ivinson Memorial Hospital by

7:04 p.m. on Wednesday, October 7, where Dr. Cantway, who was working in the emergency room at the time, determined that Matt had severe brain damage and hypothermia. Around eight o'clock, after speaking to us in Saudi Arabia, Dr. Cantway sent Matt by ambulance to Poudre Valley Hospital in Fort Collins.

The detectives couldn't tell me with certainty who they thought had attacked Matt or how he'd been attacked. But they were tracking two suspects: twenty-one-year-old men named Aaron McKinney and Russell Henderson. Both of them were from Laramie, worked as roofers in town, and had been cited in connection with another assault that had taken place early Wednesday morning, just minutes after police believe Matt was attacked. When detectives scoured McKinney's 1976 Ford pickup at the scene of that other assault, they found a Smith & Wesson .357 pistol with an eight-inch barrel that was covered in blood, a pair of shiny black shoes (which they later learned were Matt's), and an ATM card with the name Matthew Shepard on it. Everything the police found in the truck that morning seemed to suggest that, in addition to the assault they already knew about, McKinney and Henderson might have also been involved in a robbery, possibly involving someone named Matthew Shepard. But the preponderance of blood, both on the pistol and splattered around the truck, suggested that there might be more to the story than robbery. They had no hint of the severity of the other side of the story for nearly eighteen hours, until Reggie Fluty radioed in to say that she had found a young man named Matthew Shepard tethered to a fence just outside of town.

I FEEL LIKE I need to step back to say a thing or two about my state of mind at this point. I already mentioned that I thought detectives Rob DeBree and Jeff Bury were perhaps intentionally vague with me during that first visit. And I'm not certain if they did so because they wanted to protect me or because they hadn't yet connected all the dots between the two suspects and Matt and needed to protect the integrity of their case. But every word they used to provide me with an image, albeit a hazy one, of what they believed happened to Matt that night cut like a knife into my heart. At the same time, my head raced with hundreds of questions: Had those men kicked Matt? Did they use the pistol to whip him? Was he tied to that fence throughout the long cold night? With each question that tormented me, I returned to something that the neurosurgeon had told Dennis and me when we first arrived in Fort Collins: The harshest blow to Matt's head was so severe that he didn't feel pain afterward. It was weak comfort, but it was as much as I could find at that point. It helped me keep my composure and resist asking the detectives even more questions that they couldn't yet answer.

Before Rob and Jeff left, they asked if they could see Matt. When we walked into the room, I could sense that something happened in their heads. The charge was palpable. These two men had spent two nearly sleepless days gathering evidence in the case—a bank card here, a blood splatter there—and it wasn't until they saw Matt for the first time, in the hospital room that night, that they could put a face to the string of inanimate pieces of evidence and see how truly grave this case was. Only then could they see that it was a real person who had survived that heinous attack, a person with a family and friends who loved him.

When the officers prepared to head back to Laramie, Rob told me that if Matt's condition changed, he needed to know right away so that any charges pending against McKinney and Henderson could be changed to murder. I asked if it made any difference, when it came to pressing murder charges, if Dennis and I decided to stop life support. Rob didn't know. He promised to get back to me on it.

Dennis was understandably agitated when he came back from Casper without the stuffed animal he'd meant to retrieve. It didn't help that I needed to take him aside to fill him in on all the information that the detectives had given me. As usual, Dennis and I were of the same mind. As long as Matt was alive and still with us, we didn't have time to focus on the details of the attack; we needed to spend all our time with Matt.

But spending time with our son turned out to be more difficult than it should have been. Before we'd been at the hospital very long, the ICU started to fill up with friends and family members, who also wanted to see Matt. But the trouble was that the more time other loved ones spent with him, the less we were able to. We could be in the room with our family and friends at the same time if we really wanted to, but space was tight and, understanding our own desire for private time with Matt, we tried to give everybody else as much alone time as possible.

Equally tough was dealing with everyone else's viscerally emotional response to seeing Matt—a young man they'd only known as full of energy, love, enthusiasm, and wanderlust but who was now near death and in a coma. Almost without fail, Dennis and I ended up being the ones who had to console the others. I've thought about this a lot since then. During the most difficult time in our life, people turned to us for solace. I'm sure a lot of it had to do with the great pains Dennis and I were taking, for Matt's sake, to be even-keeled and in control. I doubt anybody else's emotions were as calculated or as thought-out as ours. It seemed that when people saw that Dennis and I weren't breaking down, they thought it was okay to do so themselves.

Of course it was okay. I wanted people to experience their feelings and cry if they needed to cry. It's more than likely that I would have been doing the same thing if the doctors hadn't asked that I remain upbeat.

I dealt with the stress by reminding myself how nice it was that so many people cared so much for Matt that they were driving hours through a snowstorm simply to spend time with him. Dennis, however, had more trouble with it. He's a patient man with a strong and opinionated sense of right and wrong, but when that balance goes out of whack, his patience is one of the first things to get thrown out the window. After three days without sleep and a few hours of abdicating fifteen-minute allotments of his visiting time with his son, he started to crack, getting short and angry with everyone who'd come to visit.

My husband simply couldn't understand how anybody's need to be with Matt was more important than his. I knew exactly where that feeling came from and shared a good deal of his frustration. But I also knew Dennis well enough to know that, under normal circumstances, he wouldn't have reacted that way—and he certainly wouldn't have been so quick to share his feelings with so many loved ones. After all, these people's reasons for being there were, ultimately, the same as his and mine.

I took Dennis aside for a minute to explain that these visitors were there because they loved Matt too. We needed to allow them their time with him. "This time can't be about us; it has to be about Matt," I said. "He loves these people as much as they love him. And they deserve to be able to say good-bye."

I wasn't telling Dennis anything he didn't already know. Hearing it out loud was all he needed to be set back on track. He was incredibly embarrassed that he'd cracked in the presence of so many friends and family, and he apologized for doing so.

Of course, he didn't need to apologize. If you were to talk today to any of the dozens of folks who came to visit Matt in the hospital, they'd probably tell you they didn't even know that Dennis was angry. Our friends and family members would likely say that it was surprising, considering the circumstances, that Dennis held up as well as he did. Any emotion that he showed that day was only human.

An entirely different kind of stress was the flood of media requests and the overwhelming number of well-wishers who called the hospital from all over the world. We hadn't been in Fort Collins very long before it became clear that we'd have to come up with some system to distinguish between the telephone calls we wanted to take (from people we knew) and the ones we couldn't be bothered with (from strangers, journalists, screenwriters, and politicians).

We eventually decided on a password that family and friends could use to let the hospital staff know that we wanted their telephone calls put through. The system worked, for the most part. But then one afternoon Rulon Stacey, the Poudre Valley Hospital CEO, came to tell us that a call came through from someone who he thought we'd want to talk to anyway. Dennis cut Rulon short, "No password, no call," he reminded him.

Rulon persisted. The call, he said, was from President Clinton. But Dennis, who feared that the president was only calling so he could later send out a press release, wouldn't budge. "I don't care who he is," he said. "I want to be with Matt."

Seriously, who would refuse a call from Bill Clinton? "Dennis, it's the president," I said, thinking he wasn't hearing the hospital official correctly. I, too, wanted to spend as much time with Matt as possible. But it seemed a little crazy to not take a call from the president.

Eventually Dennis agreed to accept the call under one condition—that nobody at the White House would speak to the press about it. After the call was put through, the president first talked to Dennis, expressing his sympathy to our family. Then he talked for a few minutes to Logan, who had been spending most of his time with family in the ICU waiting room. For a call that we initially didn't want to take, President Clinton's worked wonders in lifting our spirits—even just a tiny bit. Despite all the personal troubles that were riddling his administration at the time, I think he's probably one of the most compassionate men to ever make his way to Washington, D.C.

A few days later, when Dennis found out that news of Clinton's call to the hospital had somehow been leaked onto the Internet, he blew a gasket. Dennis called up a man named Richard Socarides, who was working as Clinton's liaison to the gay and lesbian community, and yelled, swore, and basically tore him a new one. I'm not sure Richard knew what to make of Dennis's anger, but he promised to do what he could to get the news off the Web and make sure no one else spoke of the telephone call. To this day, when I see Richard at fund-raising events, he laughs and says, "I want to thank your husband for the most memorable day of my life!"

Again, taking myself out of the situation and looking back at it today, I wonder why receiving a call from the president didn't make me realize the magnitude of Matt's story and its effect on people outside the hospital and outside the sphere of our immediate friends and family. But I was so focused on Matt's welfare that I was surprisingly oblivious to anything else. For example, on one of our first days in Fort Collins, Dennis and I made a special trip to buy a box of twenty-five cards to thank well-wishers. We made the purchase without thinking much beyond, "Of course, there will be a number of people to thank." We had no idea just how many people were calling and writing. We were completely unaware that there were so many plates of food, flowers, and stuffed animals being delivered to the hospital that the gifts had to be distributed to other patients. Those twenty-five cards are a stark reminder of how unprepared Dennis and I were for the attention Matt's attack would attract and how unprepared we were of the effect his story would have on people worldwide.

I ALSO DIDN'T KNOW about the candlelight vigils that were being held in cities around the world. I had no idea that Ellen DeGeneres was addressing thousands of people on the steps of the U.S. Capitol, or that four thousand people were marching on Fifth Avenue in New York City, or even that five hundred people had gathered in Matt's honor in Laramie. I'm glad that I didn't know. Acknowledging those gatherings while sequestered in the hospital would have made it even more difficult for me to answer the question that was already plaguing me: Why Matt?

I did know, however, that there was something unique about the attention the press and public were paying to Matt. In one of my first attempts to better understand the attention, I slipped out of the ICU with a friend to take part in a vigil of about a hundred people who had gathered outside the hospital. Nobody knew who I was, and I didn't introduce myself. I just wanted to know what motivated people to be there. Ultimately, I figured out that the people at the vigil that night were driven by fear and anger as much as they were by despair and sorrow for Matt. These folks knew that they could easily have been the ones who had been attacked and that they, or someone they love, might be the next to fall victim.

The scene and the sentiment were at the same time beautiful, tragic, and frustrating. Most of the people were carrying candles or posters with Matt's photo on them. Some folks had both. Where did they get that picture? I wondered. Different speakers addressed the crowd, some of them asking everyone to pray for Matt's recovery, others making a plea for a hate-crimes bill that included protections for gay people, and still others speaking out against Amendment 2, a referendum that Colorado voters had passed almost two years before, repealing antidiscrimination laws based on sexual orientation in Aspen, Denver, and Boulder.

I'd known about Matt being gay for several years, but I was more than a little out of the loop when it came to the political issues people were bringing up at the vigil that night. I'd always been a bit of a political junkie. It was something Matt and I had in common, and we'd spend hours when we were together talking about the kinds of things that would make most other people yawn: the balance of power in Congress, "most favored nation" status for China, the warring factions and ethnic cleansing in Bosnia and Herzegovina, and Osama bin Laden. Our lives in Saudi Arabia had already been affected by that man.

Living as far away as I did, in Saudi Arabia, it was easy to be out of touch with statewide measures like Amendment 2. As much as I wanted the vigil to warm my heart, it felt a little exploitive to me that night—like they were using Matt to push their own agendas. Amendment 2 had nothing to do with who Matt was, I thought. In fact, these demonstrators didn't know the first thing about who he was. I'm sure those people were devastated and horrified by what had happened to my son, but it felt like the vigil was as much for them as it was for Matt.

While I feel very differently about these gatherings now, at the time I didn't want another ounce of Matt's being—of who he really was or even who they thought he was—to be used for anything but his care. After about a half hour outside the hospital, I quietly left and returned to my own vigil at Matt's bedside.

As focused as we were on Matt and his well-being, it was impossible to completely ignore the overwhelming desire from around the world for more information about his condition. So Dennis and I started working with Rulon Stacey, the hospital's CEO, in order to release regular updates to the public. Writing press releases and organizing press conferences weren't part of Rulon's regular job, but his public relations person had quit the week before Matt was attacked. So Rulon had to take on this responsibility in addition to his regular job, and he stayed at the hospital—sleeping in his office when he got the time—in order to take care of everything.

Rulon was more compassionate, caring, and attentive than Dennis and I could have ever hoped for. In addition to ensuring that all our needs were taken care of so we could focus on Matt, Rulon also made sure that we were never bothered by the media commotion.

It was a media mob scene outside the hospital. The press

demanded regular updates, and Rulon provided them as much information as he could. On Saturday, October 10, he helped Dennis and me write our first-ever press statement, and then read it to them for us:

First of all, we want to thank the American public for their kind thoughts about Matthew and their fond wishes for his speedy recovery. We appreciate your prayers and goodwill, and we know they are something Matthew would appreciate, too.

Matthew is a very special person, and everyone can learn important lessons from his life. All of us who know Matthew see him as he is, a very kind and gentle soul. He is a strong believer in humanity and human rights. He is a trusting person who takes everybody at face value, and he does not see the bad side of anyone.

His one intolerance is when people don't accept others as they are. He has always strongly felt that all people are the same—regardless of their sexual preference, race, or religion. We know he believes that all of us are part of the same family called humanity, and each and every one of us should treat all people with respect and dignity, and each of us has the right to live a full and rewarding life. That is one lesson which we are very certain he would share with you, if he could.

At times Rulon's sensitive nature got the better of him, and he'd start to tear up while reading the report on Matt's condition. After a couple of days, he decided to discontinue the press conferences and directed the press to the hospital's Web site for updates. Not surprisingly, the site crashed within hours of his announcement.

Once when Rulon was with us in the ICU waiting room, talk turned to where we'd all gone to college. He said that he'd graduated from Brigham Young University, a school run by the Mormon Church. Because the rest of us knew the Mormon Church's official stand is that homosexuality is both immoral and unacceptable, our conversation kind of ground to a halt after Rulon's revelation. We didn't know what to make of the fact that the person who had become the de facto spokesperson for a gay kid and his very supportive family was a Mormon. I don't think anybody knew how to respond.

But then Dennis quickly turned the tables with a joke: "Well, Rulon," he said, "we're all from the University of Wyoming. We all know how UW feels about BYU when it comes to football and basketball. Let me be the first to tell you that BYU sucks!! Go Cowboys!" Suddenly the room filled with laughter. It was a moment of clarity, a moment of understanding that—whatever our lives were a week ago—we were all going through this together. Rulon and his wife have since become good friends of ours.

Rulon never let his faith stand in the way of his support

for my family when we were in the hospital. In fact, he told me that he received e-mails from church members criticizing him for being "too supportive of the gay lifestyle" in his press conferences. The fact that he was able to do his work as well as he did, and care for my family as compassionately as he did, spoke to the overwhelming sense of kindness and humanity that seemed to take hold of all of us as we cared for Matt.

AT FIRST LOGAN REFUSED TO GO into Matt's room. He was scared to death of what he'd see, and he was afraid that, if he agreed to go in the room, the sight of Matt in a coma might wipe out the image of his brother that he wanted to remember. Matt's bright-eyed, laughing, handsome face. But at one point, one of the doctors working with us strongly suggested that Dennis and I do whatever we could to get Logan into the room, suggesting that the window of opportunity was closing. The doctor advised us that Logan would likely never forgive himself if he didn't talk to Matt one more time.

So we sat down with Logan and talked with him about what he needed to do. It wasn't that he didn't want to see his brother. He just wanted to see the brother he remembered. The brother who, despite all the arguments and tussles they'd shared throughout the years, he loved more than anything. So we focused on that Matt as we talked with Logan that afternoon. We reminded Logan how relieved he'd been earlier that summer when Matt came out of the closet to him. We talked about the essay Logan had written to get into boarding school—where he outlined and expanded on all the different ways he admired his older brother and wished he could emulate him. Then we talked about how the horribly beaten-up boy in the hospital room was the same brother. He definitely didn't look the same, and he certainly couldn't talk back like he used to—but deep, deep down, he was the same Matt and he needed to know that his little brother was here with him. Logan understood, as I'm sure he always did, that he needed to go into Matt's room. And he finally agreed to do so, but only if he could be there alone with Matt.

For all our encouragement, telling Logan that he'd be okay and wouldn't regret spending time with his brother, the few minutes the two of them were in the room together turned out to be some of the most difficult of the week for all three of us. Dennis and I could see everything in Matt's room from a monitoring unit at the nurses' stations, so we posted ourselves there as Logan went in.

By then I don't think Logan was as terrified by what he thought he'd see in the room. He'd made peace with that and was trying to focus on the idea that this might be his last chance to see his brother alive. He started crying as soon as he entered the room and continued to do so for the whole fifteen minutes that he was there, touching and talking to Matt in between his sobs. We couldn't hear what he was saying, and I've never asked. But when I try to imagine the sorts of things a seventeen-year-old boy would want to say to the older brother he'd always idolized—a brother he knew he'd never get to speak to again—it rips my heart apart, just as it did that day in the nurses' station.

MATT'S CONDITION was somewhat erratic: His temperature repeatedly spiked and fell; his blood pressure would go up and down. But he never improved. He never regained consciousness—not even for a second—and never came out of his coma-induced curl, a tenseness that seemed to course through his body, making me wish that he could just let go and finally relax.

Then on Sunday night, three days after we'd arrived in Fort Collins and a couple hours after Dennis, Logan, and I had left the hospital to get some rest, we received a call from a nurse. She told us that Matt's blood pressure had grown even more erratic than it had been, and that he was starting to fail.

We rushed back to the hospital, where we met my brother, Dennis's dad, a number of family friends, and Father William Bacon, an Episcopal priest who had been with us through the week. We gathered in a circle around the hospital bed and individually said our good-byes to Matt. As I grabbed his hand and touched his forehead, I whispered to him, "Honey, it's time for you to go home."

Then, as Matt's blood pressure clearly started to take a dive for the worse, we all held each other's hands as a nurse, following our DNR request, took the ventilator tube out of his mouth. Matt immediately started to choke—as if he was trying to prove that he had a little fight left in him—and Logan nearly melted into the floor in shock. But just seconds later, everything stopped.

Matthew Wayne Shepard died at 12:53 a.m. on Monday, October 12. But our beloved, opinionated, compassionate, contentious, curious, and loving son had actually died five days earlier, tied to that fence outside Laramie.

VERY EARLY THAT MORNING, Dennis and I met with Rulon Stacey, who, at 4:30 that morning announced that Matt had died.

At 12:53 a.m. Matthew Shepard died, his family was at his bedside . . . The family did release the following statement, "We would like to thank the hospital for their kindness, professionalism, sympathy, and respect for the needs of our family under this stressful time. We will always be grateful for their concern for Matthew." The family again asked me to express their sincere gratitude to the entire world for the overwhelming response for their son. During the last twenty-four hours we have received nearly two thousand e-mails from every continent, and our Web site has received thousands of hits on Saturday and Sunday. We will continue to forward to the family any e-mail we receive . . . The family was grateful they did not have to make any decision regarding whether or not to continue life support for their son. Like a good son, he was caring to the end and removed guilt or stress from the family. He came into the world premature and left the world premature. Matthew's mother said, "Go home, give your kids a hug, and don't let a day go by without telling them you love them." Matthew's family is so grateful that his last words to them were, "I love you."

CHAPTER

Eleven

ONE OF OUR FIRST CONSIDERATIONS, immediately after Matt's autopsy, was what we wanted to do with his body.

Just as Dennis and I had been guided in the hospital by our many family conversations—especially the discussions about life support—we were fortunate enough to remember a talk we'd once had with Matt and Logan about the idea of being buried. Now, I don't want anybody to get the wrong idea; it wasn't like Dennis and I were sitting there with a legal pad and a checklist of critical "just in case" questions. Like any parents, we never ever imagined that these were issues we'd have to consider for our children. But burial had come up a couple of times with the boys while Dennis and I were trying to communicate what we wanted when our time came as well as what our parents wanted. Matt couldn't stand the idea of being put in the ground, and, to tell you the truth, I can't say I blame him. He thought it would be cold, dark, and lonely, and he never wanted to think that his future—even his future after death—might be confined to a box. He wanted to be cremated, and he wanted his ashes to be distributed somewhere special. He never said where, and Dennis and I didn't think at the time to ask.

As morose as the conversation seems in retrospect, the fact that we'd talked about it made things much easier when Dennis and I went to the funeral home in Fort Collins. There was no need to worry about what we thought Matt would have wanted, because we already knew. Thankfully, Matt's decision meant that we didn't have to go through the horrific exercise of thumbing through catalogs of caskets. Instead we selected a small oak chest with a ceramic mountain scene on top. It was lovely; it represented what Matt loved most about Wyoming— the great outdoors—and, most important, it was simple.

If I could have followed my natural inclination after Matt's death, I would have grabbed Dennis and Logan and run away— far enough away that I'd know I could protect my family. I would have gone someplace where nobody knew who we were or would want to ask us how we felt about Matt's death. However, there was too much left to do. Until now, Dennis and I had been focused on Matt's health, to the exclusion of nearly everything else. Now that Matt had passed, our focus immediately shifted to the prosecution of the men who had killed him.

So it was with that in mind that one of the first things we did after Matt died was to call detectives Rob DeBree and Jeff

Bury in Laramie, so they could change the charges leveled against Aaron McKinney and Russell Henderson to murder. Then, as soon as we finished making arrangements at the funeral home, we drove to Laramie so we could be fully briefed on the investigation. It was in a conference room at the Laramie Police Department that we first met Commander Dave O'Malley and Officer Reggie Fluty, who, together with Rob and Jeff, gave us a complete description of what the police believed had transpired on the previous Tuesday night.

By October 6, Matt had only been in school for about a month, but, true to his social nature, he was already immersed in extracurricular activities, including the university's Lesbian, Gay, Bisexual, and Transgendered Alliance (LGBTA). That night he and the other members of the alliance had gathered on campus to make the final plans for Gay Awareness Week, which was supposed to kick off with National Coming Out Day on the following Sunday. At the meeting, one of the leaders, Jim Osborn, told everyone that he'd recently been verbally harassed when he was walking across campus. Osborn later told *Vanity Fair* magazine that a guy had come up to him and said, "You're one of those faggots, aren't you?" Rather than answer, Osborn punched the harasser in the face, and the guy quickly ran away.

The alliance members were appalled, but not surprised, by Osborn's report. Homophobia wasn't rampant across campus, but they all knew it was there. While not all of them had been confronted like Osborn, most of them knew someone who had been harassed. In fact, that was exactly the purpose for their gathering that night. Their plans for Gay Awareness Week—which included a lecture by Lesléa Newman, the author of the children's book *Heather Has Two Mommies*; a screening of the movie *In & Out* starring Kevin Kline and Tom Selleck; and a discussion of "safe zones" around campus. These events were intended to help educate the larger student body about gay people and, at the same time, let closeted gay folks know that they weren't alone.

It was exactly the kind of grassroots activism that had invigorated Matt since he was a child, and I imagine that he was thrilled with the prospect of ruffling a few feathers and opening up more than a few minds with the week's planned activities. I also think Matt probably didn't want the meeting to end. He so loved the exchange of ideas and the opportunity to talk through issues with like-minded people that he was probably the one who suggested that the alliance meeting continue at the Village Inn, a diner-type restaurant a mile and a half east of campus along Grand Avenue.

After an hour of drinking coffee and sharing cherry pie at the restaurant, Matt still wasn't ready to call it a night. "He wanted to go to the Fireside [Lounge], and he begged every single one of us to go with him," an alliance member later told *The Advocate* magazine. "But it was a weeknight, and we didn't want to. We figured that he wouldn't go by himself."

However, it was early in the school year, and the other members of the LGBTA didn't know Matt well enough to know that he wouldn't hesitate to go out to a bar by himself. He'd much prefer to talk up a stranger—gay or straight—in a bar than head home alone. So after one of his friends drove him back to his apartment, Matt jumped into the Bronco and headed to the bar.

The Fireside Lounge was nothing like the Tornado Club in Fort Collins, but I understand it was the closest anything came to a gay bar in Laramie. In other words, it wasn't "gay" per se, but it tended to attract a diverse crowd, and that would have interested Matt. The bar could probably be best described as simply a college hangout—with a pool table, dartboards, dance floor, and, most important, cheap beer.

Matt arrived there by himself at about ten thirty and, as bartender Matt Galloway remembered, he sat down at the bar and ordered a Heineken. Matt wasn't a stranger to the bar, according to Galloway. He'd remembered serving him at least five or six times before that Tuesday night. Matt stood out among the bar's patrons because he was so well dressed, polite, and one of the best tippers in town, Galloway told the police. "He was one of the most polite persons I've ever met in my life."

There were only about twenty other people at the bar that night, including what looked to be a group gathered for a small birthday party. Matt pretty much stuck to himself, nursing his beer and making small talk with Galloway. "We had a very su-

perficial, 'Hey, how you doing? How has your night been?' "
the bartender said. "Both of us [said], 'Okay, good so far.' " To
Galloway it seemed that Matt wasn't at the bar for any other
particular reason other than to, "relax, kind of kick back and
have a few drinks, try not to worry . . ."

Matt was there for a little more than an hour before two
other individuals, who Galloway described as being "grungedly
dressed," came into the Fireside. Aaron McKinney and Russell
Henderson walked up to the bar and ensured that they'd stand
out from everyone else in the Fireside that night by ordering
a pitcher of beer and paying for it entirely with quarters and
dimes.

Laramie is a pretty small city—the kind people sometimes
describe as a town where "everybody knows everybody." But
Matt had only lived there for a couple of months at this point,
and there was no indication that he knew either of these other
two men. In fact, from everything I knew about Matt's life—
which, admittedly, was limited mostly to the details he wanted
to give me—he would have run in entirely different circles
from McKinney and Henderson.

Like Matt, the twenty-one-year-old McKinney was a Wyoming native. But unlike Matt, his parents (his father was a
long-haul truck driver and his mother was a nurse) divorced
when he was young. He had a number of run-ins with the law:
After flunking seventh grade, McKinney stole a cash register
and was subsequently placed in a detention center. Two years

later his mother died unexpectedly, as a result of botched surgery, and McKinney, by now a high school dropout, suddenly found himself flush with cash—nearly $100,000—as a result of a settlement in a malpractice suit related to his mother's death. The money was gone in a matter of months, though, reportedly spent on drugs, jewelry, and a sports car with the vanity license plate "Dopey," a reference to McKinney's small frame and his big ears.

As almost anyone can attest, it's a lot easier to spend a heap of money than it is to break a spending habit, and when McKinney's cash was gone, he turned to robbery again, stealing twenty-five hundred dollars and some desserts from a local Kentucky Fried Chicken during December 1997, ten months before the attack on Matt. He'd moved to Florida to escape sentencing for the robbery charge but came back to Laramie after police tracked him down, moving into a run-down one-bedroom apartment with his girlfriend, Kristen Price, and their infant son, Cameron. McKinney was working as a roofer and awaiting sentencing on charges related to the fast-food robbery when he walked into the Fireside that night.

Henderson, too, was raised in Wyoming. Like McKinney, he was a twenty-one-year-old who'd had a less-than-ideal childhood: Raised by a single mother, who reportedly had a drinking problem, he was removed from her house and placed with his maternal grandmother.

By all accounts, Henderson flourished under the care

of his grandmother, who was a devout Mormon. He was an honor student, a member of the Future Farmers of America, and even became an Eagle Scout. To meet the requirements for that last honor, Henderson cleaned a local cemetery and, as a result, had his picture taken with the governor of Wyoming and printed in Laramie's newspaper, the *Boomerang*. But that trajectory of success somehow veered off course after Henderson turned seventeen. He dropped out of high school, moved out of his grandmother's home, and started to hang out with folks like McKinney. Soon he, too, had a police record, including two arrests for drunk driving and a third for fighting with a police officer.

Henderson, who had once worked at Taco Bell with McKinney, and had most recently worked with him as a roofer, lived in a mobile home with his girlfriend, Chastity Pasley, a student at the university.

After McKinney and Henderson emptied their pockets for the pitcher of beer at the Fireside, Galloway remembered that they headed to the back of the bar, where they hung out mostly by the pool table. The bartender wasn't sure how they'd ended up talking with Matt—whether Matt approached them first or the other way around. Knowing Matt and his ease with making conversation with strangers, I wouldn't be surprised if he was the first to extend his hand, perhaps when he was walking past the pool table on his way to or from the bathroom. However it happened, police believe that once Henderson and McKinney learned that Matt was gay—whether because he told them or because they simply guessed—they devised a plan to rob him.

Also a bit of the mystery is how they coaxed Matt into McKinney's '76 Ford pickup. The police suggested that Henderson and McKinney's robbery plan included pretending that they were gay, in order to gain Matt's confidence, and then suggesting a sexual hookup with him. But I think it's just as likely that Matt, who, by Galloway's account, had consumed three drinks by this point, thought he was too drunk to drive and accepted a ride home from the other men.

It was between 11:45 p.m. and midnight when both Galloway and the bouncer at the Fireside saw Matt leave the bar with Henderson and McKinney. They all got into the cab of McKinney's black pickup. Henderson was in the driver's seat, McKinney in the passenger's seat, and Matt sat between the two of them. Despite the obvious differences between the three men, nobody took much note of them leaving together. Laramie was the kind of place where dissimilar people always seemed to cross paths and mingle with each other. This was especially the case at a bar like the Fireside.

The trio didn't head to Matt's apartment, which was only a dozen blocks away. And they didn't make their way toward McKinney's place or Henderson's either. Instead they took a roundabout route (which police attribute to the fact that neither Henderson nor McKinney had a valid driver's license and didn't want to get pulled over) to the east side of town—past the string of businesses and homes that had popped up between the center of town and the Wal-Mart on the far east side of Laramie.

McKinney later told police that Matt tried to hit on him while they were in the truck—putting his hand on McKinney's leg, grabbing his crotch, and even trying to lick his ear. (Henderson, however, told police that he saw none of this.) When the truck approached the Wal-Mart complex, McKinney announced, "Guess what? We're not gay, and you're getting jacked," and he then ordered Matt to hand over his wallet, which had only twenty dollars in it.

Later, when he was recounting the night in his discussions with police, McKinney couldn't remember if he first struck Matt with his fist or with the butt of his Smith & Wesson .357 pistol, which had an eight-inch barrel. But he told police that it wasn't the small amount of money that set him off—it was the fact that Matt was hitting on him so hard. It's a claim that, after much contemplation, I find difficult to believe. After all, how surprised could McKinney have been if Matt really had been hitting on him, especially after he and Henderson, by their own admission, had pretended to be gay in order to lure Matt into the truck in the first place?

Regardless of the provocation, McKinney pounded Matt in the face, neck, and chest. And as he did, Henderson kept driving for a mile or so past Wal-Mart and through a subdivision called Imperial Heights. Then, at the dead end of a paved road called Palomino Drive, he continued for about another four hundred yards along a worn dirt path until he was blocked by both a slight depression in the land and a split-rail fence.

Only then did Henderson turn off the truck and give his attention to McKinney, who by this time was trying to drag Matt out of the truck. Matt fought back, kicking McKinney hard in the chest. Still, as scrappy as he was and as strong willed as he'd always been when confronted with problems much bigger than he'd ever be, Matt was no match for two men, especially not after he'd already been bloodied up in the truck cab.

McKinney succeeded in getting Matt out of the truck and to the ground, where he continued to punch him, kick him, and wallop him with the butt of the pistol. Henderson, according to his friend McKinney, just stood by and laughed.

Screaming for mercy, Matt begged McKinney to stop. He even tried to negotiate for his life, telling him and Henderson that there was $150 in his apartment that they could have if they would just let him be. But still with his wits about him, Matt tried to trick his attackers by giving them an address other than his own. I think he was hoping McKinney and Henderson wouldn't be able to get away with what they had done if they went to someone else's address looking for his apartment.

The offer didn't persuade McKinney to ease up. He continued to strike Matt as he ordered Henderson to get some rope from the back of the truck. When Henderson returned with some white clothesline, McKinney demanded that he tie Matt to the fence. The former Eagle Scout did as he was told, tying Matt's hands behind his back (with the backs of his hands facing each other) and then to the fence. Only at that point, Henderson later told police, did he realize how much trouble he'd gotten himself into, and—in a move that I assume was more out of concern for his own welfare than out of any sympathy for Matt—he said he asked his friend to stop.

But McKinney wouldn't. Instead, as Henderson described, McKinney turned his wrath, if only for a second, away from Matt and toward his accomplice, striking Henderson hard on the lip with the butt of the gun. That was the end of Henderson's revolt. He later told the police that he didn't do any more to help Matt because "I was afraid what happened to Matt Shepard would happen to me."

McKinney also began to worry, not for Matt or Henderson, though, but about the likelihood that he'd get caught for what he'd just done. He started to talk with Matt, who was now sitting tied to the foot of the fence, telling him that he was from California in the hope that Matt might pass on the misinformation to the police. Then, just as the rapists in Marrakech had done to Matt three and a half years before, McKinney took off Matt's shoes and threw them in his truck. He later told police that he took the shoes so he could be sure that if, by some amazing feat, Matt was able untie himself from the fence, he'd have difficulty walking the four miles home.

But even that wasn't enough to calm McKinney's fear of getting caught. So finally, just to be on the safe side, he asked Matt if he could read the license plate on his truck. The still-headstrong Matt said he could and then read the letters and numbers back, "665AD," to his attacker. Matt's defiance sent McKinney over the edge, and in that moment he made a calculated decision to ensure that Matt would never be able to talk to the police about this attack. He struck him hard—once, twice, and a third time—with the butt of the pistol. The blows crushed Matt's skull, essentially caving it in behind his ear on the right side of his head, and knocked him unconscious. From everything we learned from the neurologist in Fort Collins, it was those three blows that ended Matt's life, putting him in a coma, making him completely unconscious and unaware of his surroundings.

For all the lives that have been forever changed by the heinous acts committed on the outskirts of Laramie in the early hours of October 7—and as significant a scar as it left on the psyche of the entire country—the ordeal lasted less than forty-five minutes. McKinney, Henderson, and Matt left the Fireside Lounge at about 11:45 p.m., at the earliest. A Wyoming state trooper who lives in the Imperial Heights section of town reported that he saw a truck matching the description of McKinney's leave the dirt path near Palomino Drive and head back toward town between 12:26 and 12:30 a.m.

Considering that, by the police's estimation, it takes approximately six minutes to get from the bar to Wal-Mart and another ten minutes to get from Wal-Mart to the fence, Henderson and McKinney were at the fence for only about twenty-five minutes before they got back into the pickup and left Matt tied to the fence to die. In other words, it probably took less time for these men to kill my son than it took them, just hours before, to gather their loose change, drive to the bar, and buy a pitcher of beer.

The night was far from over, though. After leaving Matt behind, Henderson and McKinney made a beeline for downtown Laramie. It's not clear whether they were trying to sell the pistol (which is what they later said they had planned to do that evening before meeting Matt at the bar) or heading for the fake address Matt had given them in order to steal the $150 Matt said he had stashed there. But for some reason they stopped at the intersection of Seventh and Harney streets, where they encountered Jeremy Herrera and Emiliano Morales, two young men who were prowling the business district and vandalizing cars. As Herrera and Morales were slashing tires, they came face-to-face with Henderson and McKinney, who by this time had gotten out of the truck and were walking down the street.

The four of them apparently exchanged pleasantries at first, but, as might be expected when petty vandals run into would-be murderers in the middle of the night, the conversation quickly went downhill. "We were cussing back and forth to each other and FU, bitches, and stuff like that," Herrera later explained. Then, before he and Morales knew it, McKinney had run back to his truck and pulled out the pistol again. Next he whacked Morales on the head with it. "It was the most sickening thud I ever heard in my life," Herrera said, describing the sound the butt of the gun made as it hit his friend's head. "Kind of like when you hit something wooden, and it's like a thunk. Thunk like that. I heard it from almost ten feet away. It was just . . . I don't know; it kind of made me sick to my stomach when I first heard it."

What McKinney didn't know was that Herrera had a weapon of his own—a whittled piece of wood that was about sixteen inches long and about as wide as the small end of a bat. When Herrera saw what McKinney did to his friend, he pulled out the club and struck hard against McKinney's own head.

After receiving what must have amounted to little more than a hint of the viciousness he'd dealt Matt, McKinney retreated.

At 12:43 a.m. Officer Flint Waters of the Laramie Police Department received a call regarding possible vandalism around Seventh and Harney streets. But rather than run into Herrera and Morales when he reported to the scene, he saw McKinney and Henderson jumping back into McKinney's truck. "I saw that both of them had blood on them," the officer said. "The driver had blood around his mouth [and] the man on the passenger's side had blood on the side of his head."

Officer Waters, who runs the department's K-9 unit, had no sooner started to announce his presence over his patrol car's public-address system—"Stop, or I'll release the dog"—than McKinney and Henderson bolted away from the truck in opposite directions. Following protocol, Waters chased the suspect, Henderson, who he believed to be the truck's driver, and overtook him and had him handcuffed within a few minutes.

Noticing a crescent-shaped gash above Henderson's lip, Waters first called for an ambulance and then read Henderson his Miranda rights before arresting him on charges of interfering with a police officer.

"He started to tell me that he and a friend had come to the area looking for a party, and that they had been jumped by two guys," Waters said. "He then told me that we should be looking for those two guys."

Then, perhaps because Henderson remembered that several people had seen him leave the Fireside with McKinney and Matt earlier that night, Henderson, Waters said, added to his story: " 'Well, there were three of us and the third friend went looking for this party, and me and my second friend waited in the truck. The third friend didn't come back, we went out looking for him, and that's when we got jumped.' "

A little after one, after an ambulance rushed Henderson away to the hospital, Waters went back to examine the truck.

As he approached the driver's side of the cab, he saw something on the ground that upon closer inspection he recognized as a pistol rug, a cloth pouch where handguns are stored. "I grabbed my radio, and I immediately broadcast to all the officers searching the area," he said. "I broadcast that [McKinney] may be armed. It was a big deal, critical for us.

"I obviously had something bigger than I had originally anticipated. I started walking down the rest of the truck. I looked over in the back of the truck, and lying in the back of the truck was a big pistol with a hammer cocked back, and it was covered in blood."

Waters rushed to the hospital to question Henderson again, and Henderson repeated the same story he'd recited when he and Waters were waiting for the ambulance. He didn't flinch when confronted with news about the gun. "I don't know nothing about no gun," he told Waters several times.

Despite any hunches Waters had, he didn't have enough evidence to keep Henderson in custody. So when Henderson mentioned that he thought his girlfriend, Chastity Pasley, might be worried about him, Waters called Pasley to tell her that her boyfriend was in the emergency room.

"I said [to Chastity], I'm at the hospital with Russell. He is going to be okay," Waters remembered. "And she said, 'Aaron's girlfriend called. Is Aaron going to be okay?' " With that, Waters and the police were able to tie Aaron McKinney to whatever had happened that night.

Waters recalled the conversation with Henderson at the hospital, as well: "[I] went back to the treatment room [and] told [Henderson] I talked to his girlfriend, and I said she asked about Aaron. I said, 'So it was Aaron you were with?' He said, 'Yeah, since you already know, I was with Aaron McKinney.' I told him that I was finishing up the ticket and I needed him to sign it. He asked me again, 'Are you going to let me go tonight?' I said, 'Yeah, I got some guys out there looking around; if they find somebody out there with a bullet in them, we are going to have to visit you and Aaron.'

"He started laughing and said, 'I guarantee you are not going to find anybody with a bullet in them.' And he looked up and down, and said it again."

Among the other men out there looking for clues were Officer Mitchell Cushman and Commander Dave O'Malley, both of the Laramie Police Department. Cushman, who had been part of the initial team searching for the vandals, was among the officers responsible for documenting the evidence in McKinney's truck, including the .357 Magnum. In addition to the pistol, they found Matt's shoes, size-seven Bed/Stüs, and Henderson's Boss-brand jacket.

"This particular truck reminded me of a ranch truck just because of the things that were in the back. It had grass on the bumper. It was kind of dirty," Cushman later said in trial testimony. "It was kind of unusual to me to have a pair of—like, this low-cut, shiny loafer in the middle of a ranch-type pickup truck.

That was one of the things I noted. I did not confiscate this, but there was one shoe [on the seat] and one on the floor."

On the dash, they found a Hilltop National Bank card with the name Matthew Shepard on it, leading police to believe that they were dealing with a robbery of some sort.

But most notable was the blood. It was everywhere—on the pistol, on Henderson's jacket, and throughout the truck cabin. "At that point in time, we were totally unaware of anything else that had occurred," Dave O'Malley later said. "But we surmised that something else had occurred due to the amount of blood."

Henderson's girlfriend, twenty-year-old Chastity Pasley, was a student at the University of Wyoming and worked part time in the Student Union Building, assisting student groups. In fact, she'd most likely been working with the LGBTA as it prepared for Gay Awareness Week. Yet when she learned, after picking Henderson up from the hospital, that he and McKinney had beaten up a gay guy and left him somewhere out past Wal-Mart, she did nothing.

Before going to the hospital, Pasley stopped by the apartment McKinney shared with his girlfriend, nineteen-year-old Kristen Price, and their toddler son, Cameron. Price told Pasley that McKinney had already stumbled home, bleeding from a huge gash in his head, and had declared that he and Henderson had killed someone. So when she, Price, and Cameron arrived at the hospital, Pasley immediately asked Henderson

what had happened. He confirmed that they'd roughed someone up, and even that they'd left that person out in a field
on the east side of town, but said that McKinney didn't know
what he was talking about and, as Pasley later recalled, that
their victim "was going to be okay."

From the hospital, Pasley drove back to the trailer home
she and Henderson shared, because she was afraid she'd left
the front door unlocked. (It baffles me today to think that,
with all that was going on that early morning, an unlocked
door was what concerned her most.) After checking on the
trailer, she then drove back to McKinney's apartment, where
the four of them conspired about what they'd say about the
previous night if they were questioned by police.

"Russ and Aaron were going to say somebody took [Mc-
Kinney's] truck and then they were taking him [Matthew] to
a party over by La Bonte Park, and that is how they ended
up there and that somebody came and jumped them," Pasley
said.

The next morning, Pasley went back to work and class as if
nothing had happened.

Kristen Price, on the other hand, seemed a little more concerned about what might be going on. McKinney was covered
in blood when he arrived back at their apartment that night,
and he told Price that he thought he'd killed someone, and
that she should turn off all the lights and the TV and come
into the bathroom to talk with him.

Once they were both in the bathroom, Price said that McKinney started to wash blood off what appeared to be a wallet and its contents—a driver's license, a voter card, and a Dairy Queen coupon—and then tried to explain to Price what had happened.

"He said that he and Russell went to the bar, and that they had met someone there, and he was a gay guy and was hitting on him. I don't know, asking him out. I don't know. He said that it was when he and Russell went to the bathroom and decided to pretend they were gay and get him in the truck and rob him."

Although McKinney had a tendency to exaggerate, as she remembered, Price worried—especially with all the blood—that McKinney might be telling the truth this time, that he might have really killed this gay guy. So she, too, asked Henderson about it after she and Pasley picked him up from the hospital.

"Russell assured me that everything was fine," she said. "He said, 'Believe me. He's okay. Aaron's just exaggerating. Don't worry about it.' So I trusted him, and I thought everything was going to be fine."

But still there was all that blood, and McKinney himself appeared to be badly injured. He was having an increasing amount of difficulty talking straight as a result of his head wound. So by four the next afternoon, October 7, when Detective Ben Fritzen showed up at her front door looking for McKinney and telling her that her boyfriend was in trouble and that the police needed to talk with him, Price started to worry again.

She told Fritzen that she didn't know where her boyfriend was, but as soon as the officer left, she went to the bedroom, where McKinney was sleeping, and told him she was going to call the cops. "I didn't want to go to jail, and I didn't want to lose Cameron," she later explained.

So she called Jeff Bury, who had left a card on McKinney's truck, and left a message informing him that McKinney had returned home and that she was taking him to the hospital. "I told [Jeff] if he wanted to, he could meet me there, and if not, I would take Aaron wherever he wanted me to take him."

About an hour and a half after Price took her boyfriend to the hospital, and a full eighteen hours after McKinney and Henderson left Matt to die, eighteen-year-old Aaron Kreifels came barreling out of nearby Cactus Canyon on his mountain bike, heading toward the highway so he could make it back to his dorm room before dark. In his haste he hit a rock, took a spill, and caught sight of Matt, who was still unconscious and tethered to the fence after spending nearly a full day— including a night with near-freezing temperatures—out there on his own.

"At first I couldn't believe that it could be a person up there," Kreifels said later. "I thought it was a Halloween guy. It looked like a scarecrow. I grabbed my bike and walked near to check it out, and I noticed he was breathing very hard. It sounded to me like his lungs might be filled with blood. I'm not sure, but that is what it sounded like. He was breathing very hard."

Understandably shaken by what he'd found, Aaron ran to the nearest house, about 250 yards south of where Matt was, and asked the home's owner, university professor Charles Dolan, to call 911. Then Charles and Aaron ran back to where Matt was and waited for the police to arrive.

"When I walked up to him, I asked could he hear—could he respond to any talking; he couldn't. I touched him on the shoulder and couldn't get any response," Charles said. "I listened to his breathing. His breathing was—I could tell that it was labored, but you've heard someone who is really sound asleep—it's a deep breathing followed by an exhale."

It took a full twenty minutes before Sheriff's Deputy Reggie Fluty made it to the scene. "When I arrived there, I saw part of somebody lying down," Reggie later recounted. "As I approached, I could see that this—it was a young male. He looked very young, probably thirteen, fourteen years old. Real small stature. Large pool of blood underneath his head, and I noticed that most of the blood was just underneath his head."

Reggie juggled several responsibilities as she waited for an ambulance to arrive to take Matt to the hospital. Of course, her primary focus was to make sure Matt stayed alive. First she asked Charles if he could help her turn Matt on his side (he was lying on his back with his arms tied behind him), so that she could cut the ropes that bound him to the fence. But when they moved Matt to his left side, he stopped breathing. So they immediately rolled him onto his back again and tipped his jaw slightly back, and then he started breathing again.

Reggie also secured the scene of what she automatically knew had been a crime. And in doing so, she found, among other things, a University of Wyoming ID with Matt's name on it and a watch—a Raymond Weil watch Dennis and I bought Matt for his high school graduation. The band was snapped, suggesting that it had been pulled off during a struggle.

Then, after the ambulance came and rushed Matt to the Laramie hospital, Reggie returned a call to Jeff Bury, who'd been trying to reach her on the radio. "He asked me [if] Matthew was related to this aggravated assault he had earlier, and I said, 'I'm sorry. I don't know what your aggravated assault was.' I said I had a subject here who has been tied and severely beaten about the head. I said, 'I have a UW card here. The first name is Matthew,' and [then] Detective Bury said, 'Shepard.' "

MATT WASN'T the only patient in the emergency room when he arrived at Ivinson Memorial Hospital on that Wednesday night. In fact, he wasn't the only patient in the emergency room suffering from head trauma. Aaron McKinney was there as well, and he and Matt were both being treated by Dr. Cantway, who later said that—counting Emiliano Morales, who had been in the emergency room about fifteen hours earlier—he'd never before seen a time when the hospital had to deal with so many head injuries in a twenty-four-hour period.

Within an hour after Matt was admitted, Dr. Cantway determined that the hospital in Laramie wasn't equipped to deal with either Matt's or McKinney's injuries, so he sent them both—in separate ambulances—to Fort Collins, where, again, they were treated by the same neurosurgeon.

I've had many conversations with Dennis and Logan—as well as with Rob DeBree, Jeff Bury, Dave O'Malley, and Reggie Fluty—since that day after Matt's death, when we all met for the first time to discuss the details of the murder. We've all agreed that, at the time, it felt like all of us—including Matt, McKinney, and Henderson—were pieces in a big board game, being moved around by some higher power. When we stopped to think about it, too many things happened on the day of my son's attack that were unlikely to have transpired in the normal, logical stream of life. Matt's bad luck in meeting McKinney and Henderson in the first place was followed quickly by the police officer noticing McKinney's truck as he and Henderson headed back to town after beating Matt. Then McKinney and Henderson running into Herrera and Morales downtown, Officer Waters catching Henderson when he thought he was chasing one of the suspected vandals, and Aaron Kreifels hitting the rock and taking a tumble where he could see Matt tied to the fence. Next the bank card found on the dash in McKinney's truck helped police connect the dots quickly. And then there was the surreal fact that Matt and his murderer were treated simultaneously, in two different hospitals, by the same doctors, who at the time had no idea how the two men were connected.

It's not that I think Matt was meant to be murdered or that Henderson and McKinney were driven by anything other than their own hatred when they killed my son. That's certainly not the case. It's just that, after things went so horribly off track that night—in that typical local bar in that typical American town—it seemed to all of us that somebody, something, or some power stepped in to, as much as possible, set things right.

Reggie later told me a story about when she first saw Matt tied to the fence that only further underscores my feelings about involvement of a higher power. Reggie said that as she ran to the fence she saw a large doe lying near Matt—as if the deer had been keeping him company through the night. "I didn't see her until I started running up," she said of the deer. "Like the old saying—'deer in the headlights'—the doe looked right at me, and *poom!* She was outta there. Matthew couldn't talk to me. He had been exposed for most of the night and half a day. Even though I tried to comfort him and let him know somebody was there, I think his comfort came from that big old doe. That was the good Lord, no doubt in my mind. I'm sure he could feel her and she could feel him, and she was with him till help came."

In the face of all the gruesome details the police outlined for us, Reggie's story comforted me. It made me feel better to hear that Matt might not have been alone during all those hours while he was tied to that fence, fighting for his life. But the only way I've been able to keep my composure and, really, my sanity—whether during the day in the hospital when Jeff and Rob first outlined what they thought had happened to Matt, or when the Laramie Police Department officers gave us a fuller account of the evidence they'd gathered, or even today when someone asks me a question about the night Matt was attacked—is by fighting every temptation to "go there" in my head. I can't make any attempt to visualize the circumstances of Matt's murder. I've never been to the spot where he was attacked or tried, in any way, to share in the experience of that horrible night. Sure, I cried, and I still do, usually when I'm alone. To do it in public seems counterproductive. It was—and still is—critical to me that people pay attention to Matt and what happened to him, but not to me.

AFTER LEAVING THE POLICE STATION, I told Dennis I had one more difficult errand. I wanted to stop at Matt's apartment. I needed to find something that would make me feel like he was with me at the memorial service.

Going through Matt's belongings in his Laramie apartment was a decidedly more difficult process than talking to the police had been. In retrospect, I think I must have known that this task wouldn't be easy. We'd been to Matt's apartment just months before. It best represented Matt's life the way it had been before he went to the Fireside Lounge on that fateful Tuesday night. In fact, aside from a little disorder left by the detectives who searched it for a link between Matt and his murderers, the apartment was exactly as Matt had left it.

I didn't expect that we'd run into difficulty before we even got into Matt's place, though. As we parked, I noticed that there was a CNN van in front of the apartment building. Then, as Dennis and I walked toward the front door, a TV reporter and cameraman got out of the vehicle and started to walk toward us. Incredibly, considering the overwhelming media attention Matt's case had been receiving, it was the first time either Dennis or I had come face-to-face with a journalist. Seeing them come my way, I immediately panicked, both out of fear that they were going to ask me to put words to the pain I'd just been through and disgust that reporters would even dare do that. I'd only been able to get through the previous week in the same way I've been able to get through every day since that week—by keeping my emotions in check. But there was no way I'd be able to keep my composure, to keep myself from going there, if someone started pelting me with questions, especially those that were designed to make me cry. They didn't care so much about how I felt and weren't

so interested in hearing the details of what Dennis and I had
been through since Matt's attack. Journalists just wanted to
see us, the grieving parents, cry. That's what they needed
to set their coverage apart from every other report; it's why
they were parked in front of Matt's apartment, waiting for
God knows how long on the off chance that Dennis and I
would show up. It felt like such an incredible invasion of our
privacy.

"They're coming this way," I whispered to Dennis as the
reporters got closer. Then, before I could turn around and
go back to the car, one of them extended the microphone instead of his hand. Dennis pushed me behind him before looking at the reporter, shaking his head, and calmly saying, "Not
today."

I couldn't believe it at the time, but that's all it took; the
CNN team quietly and respectfully retreated back into their
van. Still, those reporters stuck in my head for a long time.
I appreciate that they had a job to do. I also understand that
they had no way of knowing Dennis's or my state of mind—
that I'd just taken my twenty-one-year-old son to be cremated,
and before that, that I had been briefed on the details of his
murder. But, especially in cases like these, I just can't help but
think that there should be boundaries, inherent if not tacitly
implied, to protect the privacy of the grieving family. When
those reporters saw me behind my husband, it shouldn't have
taken Dennis saying "Not today" for them to know that this

wasn't the right time to stick a microphone or TV camera in my face.

I'm not sure what we expected to find inside Matt's place. Perhaps, like the police who'd been there before us, Dennis and I were looking for answers, anything to help explain the unexplainable. But just as the detectives found nothing in the apartment to link Matt to Henderson or McKinney, we really didn't find any answers we were looking for either.

What was most striking was just how normal everything appeared once we stepped through the door. The world was clamoring for information, for anything new they could learn about Matthew Shepard, an angelic-looking gay kid who had just died after being strung to a fence outside town. But this is where our son, a run-of-the-mill college kid named Matt, had lived. He wasn't a saint, as the press was trying to make him out to be, but a twenty-one-year-old with more troubles than anyone his age should ever have to deal with. Yet as I looked around his apartment that day, it was clear to me that by simply living his life and going to school Matt was doing his best to overcome his demons.

The apartment was a bit of a mess, but Matt had never been very tidy. His fridge and cupboards were pretty close to bare, save for a few snacks, ramen and Cup Noodles–type foods, but Matt much preferred to grab dinner at a coffee shop or diner with a friend than to eat alone at home. There were a ton of clothes though. We found button-down shirts that I remembered buying during our trip to London five years before, baseball caps he'd worn for years, and piles of oversize threads—standard-issue college slouch wear, I suppose—that he must have picked up at secondhand stores over the years.

The textbooks and notebooks we found in the apartment were the biggest indication to me that Matt had been making a real point of getting his life back on track. Unlike his previous stabs at college life in North Carolina and Casper, it was clear from the highlighted passages in his texts and the spiral notebooks that he had started to fill with notes that he was actually attending class this time, which marked real progress.

The various cold remedies we found strewn around the apartment suggested that there had been another battle on the horizon, one that Matt didn't yet know had taken hold of his life. If he'd lived, it may have become the most difficult battle he'd ever face.

When I first saw the cold medicine, I remembered the last time we spoke Matt told me that he wasn't feeling well and that he thought he might be coming down with something. Then I recalled what the doctor in Fort Collins told us when we asked about the possibility of donating Matt's organs. He was HIV positive and based on the level of virus present in his blood, it looked like his was a recent infection. Though I knew very little about HIV at the time, I remembered hearing that HIV-positive people often feel flulike symptoms soon after they're infected.

All this confirmed what I had already assumed. Matt didn't know he'd been infected, and the cold medicine suggested that he was on the verge of facing the telltale symptoms. Had my son lived, the diagnosis would have devastated him. It's hard to say if learning about his HIV status might have hampered his mental state and strengthened his depression. I'd like to think that it might have served as a motivating force, making him more diligent about going to therapy and continuing to attend class on a regular basis. I also hope that he'd have stuck with his plan to pursue a career in international relations. We would have learned, as a family, that HIV is no longer the death sentence it once was and that, as long as Matt took care of his health, saw his doctor on a regular basis, and took his medication as prescribed, it most likely wouldn't stand in the way of his dreams, goals, and ambitions. That's how I hope things would have transpired, but, of course, I'll never know.

CHAPTER

Twelve

IT SNOWED SO HARD on Friday, October 16, the day of Matt's memorial service, that people in Casper still refer to the "October Storm." In the city park across the street from St. Mark's Episcopal Church, where we held the service, the trees were so overburdened by the weight of the snowfall that their branches came crashing down. Later, throughout Casper, dozens of other giant cottonwoods had to be cut down. And for me, the still-small replacement trees are as much a reminder of that day as my memories of the memorial service itself.

What can one say—that hasn't already been said—about the pain of burying a child? It feels almost cliché when I tell people that it's the most difficult thing I've ever experienced. Maybe that's because the statement isn't quite true; it was much more excruciating to see Matt in the ICU for the first time, and then imagining the pain he must have been put through before he arrived at the hospital. Compared to the agony of the days before it, preparing for the memorial service felt more like a hazy process—something we just needed to get through in order to get on with more pressing matters, like prosecuting Matt's killers.

In all honesty, Dennis and I didn't have to deal with the details of the service; Dennis's brother and sister-in-law, and my brother, took care of all of that for us. But their generosity didn't leave us completely without chores and responsibility.

My parents didn't have me baptized as a baby. They left it up to me to decide what church I wanted to attend (if any). I appreciated the freedom and decided to take the same approach when it came time to raise my own kids. Matt eventually joined my church—St. Mark's Episcopal Church in Casper—and we attended services together on a regular basis when we lived there. Logan, on the other hand, never took much interest in church. Even though he and his dad would join Matt and me on occasional Sunday mornings, they much preferred to stay home to watch the ball games.

I bring this up now to explain why we chose St. Mark's as the location for Matt's memorial services. Matt hadn't attended services very often since we moved to Saudi Arabia, but it was a church he chose for himself as a youngster, a place where he'd always been comfortable while growing up. In terms of the actual planning for the service, it helped that my brother was also a longtime member of St. Mark's Church. He, Dennis's sister-in-law, and Dennis's brother took care of everything. In fact, Dennis and I gave them only one direction: "Do what you think is best. We're sure it will be beautiful."

Their very gracious help left Dennis and me with the time to worry about the sorts of things that nobody should have to think about for a memorial service, such as where to accommodate all the people who wanted to attend and how to make sure that the folks who mattered most to Matt were able to get into the sanctuary. By Wednesday, two days before the memorial service, it was clear that what was supposed to be a solemn celebration of Matt's life ran the terrible risk of turning into a three-ring circus. CNN wanted to carry the services live, but we quickly denied the request. Instead we agreed to let a local radio station broadcast it, primarily because the radio feed could be played for people outside. It could also be heard in neighboring churches, where we expected the overflow crowds to gather. There were also calls from the White House and Capitol Hill, from Desmond Tutu and the archbishop of Canterbury—a combination of well-wishes and requests to send representatives to the service. While we appreciated the sentiment, we couldn't understand why anyone who never knew Matt would want to attend his memorial services. I think we then realized that all this was about more than Matt. It was also about the senseless violence and hate that ended his life.

But Dennis and I couldn't think about that, especially when we were occupied with shielding Logan from the chaos. We also had to worry about whether there'd be enough room for all our loved ones to attend the services. As crazy as it sounds, we had to resort to putting together a guest list, as well as print and issue tickets. We had to make sure the people who mattered most to us and Matt weren't excluded because of strangers.

We were also painfully aware of the strain that all this commotion was placing upon our hometown and our home state. I'd never suggest that Wyoming was the most accepting or open-minded place on earth, but there was no way that the entire state, or its residents, deserved to be painted by the same broad brush the media was using when discussing McKinney, Henderson, and the circumstances that led to Matt's murder. I'd lived in Wyoming my whole life and knew as well as anyone that McKinney and Henderson didn't represent the city of Laramie, the state of Wyoming, or the people who live there. Still, I worried about how these generalizations would hurt my friends and neighbors and feared that their frustration might translate into anger with Matt and with the rest of our family.

I should have known better. It took my breath away when I walked into St. Mark's the day before the memorial service and saw dozens of women from the church's Altar Guild volunteering their time to clean every inch of the sanctuary. I can never thank them enough. I'd never seen the church look that beautiful before.

I was similarly overwhelmed when my hometown paper came out with an editorial denouncing the kind of hatred that led to Matt's murder. "Prejudice against homosexuals is just as redneck as anti-black bias," the editors at the *Casper Star-Tribune* wrote. "Violence against our homosexual friends and neighbors has created a most un-American climate of fear in Wyoming and the rest of the nation."

Jason Marsden, who was a friend of Matt's and a reporter at the *Star-Tribune* at the time, wrote a beautifully poignant column, in which he came out of the closet as a gay man and called for everyone to look beyond the news—and to the bigger lesson in Matt's murder:

What happened here in Wyoming this week makes good news. But it must be more than news. It must be a clarion call to our fragmented 20th-century souls. To recover our heritage of love and cast off the slavery that hatred subjects us to. Hatred will always target light. Their feud predates time itself. Let us hope, and pray, and fight like hell to see that this tragedy does not come to represent our state and our unique community. Each of us has the power to prevent that. How? By being a little more like Matt. Open. Loving. And maybe even—like we "country cousins" are in the stereotype of the outside world—a little too trusting for our own good.

Businesses in Casper started putting posters up in their storefront windows that resembled the yellow ribbon with green circles (yellow for tolerance and green for peace) that were popping up at the University of Wyoming. Suddenly in this live-and-let-live state, where I'd always assumed that it was okay to be gay as long as you didn't tell anyone, people were taking a stand, and they were saying that things needed to change. In our hometown, in our church, and at our alma mater, people were standing up for our son—and for our family. And, for the first time that week, I felt so blessed.

IF ONLY EVERYONE had been so loving.

Like most Americans, I had never heard of the Reverend Fred Phelps or his Westboro Baptist Church out of Topeka, Kansas, before October 1998, and I don't think either Dennis or I knew what to make of the news that Phelps and his parishioners would be protesting Matt's memorial service. "Protesting?" we asked, seriously perplexed by the notion that anyone could find anything to protest in a memorial service. After all, we were just paying tribute and saying good-bye to our son. Nothing more, nothing less.

As I later learned, the Westboro Baptist Church wasn't really a church—at least not in the traditionally accepted definition of the word. It was a group made up primarily of Phelps's family members, who, rather than preaching love and forgiveness, traveled the country protesting gay pride events and memorial services of AIDS victims with their now infamous "God Hates Fags" picket signs. According to articles I've read, Phelps's estranged son claims that the church subsists—

and makes a lot of the money required for its cross-country protests—from lawsuits it files against people who are provoked to respond in one way or another to the picket signs and the chants promising that gay people will "rot in hell." I suppose that Phelps and his clan must have seen an opportunity in Matt's memorial service—a chance to, for the first time, attract the ire of hundreds of thousands of folks at the same time. In the years since Matt's memorial service, the Westboro Baptist Church has broadened its scope to picket the funerals of fallen soldiers from the war in Iraq.

It probably helped that Phelps and his asinine ways came to our attention during a week when absolutely nothing made sense. We already had too much to worry about, so we wasted as little time as possible thinking about what this clan might do in its despicable ploy for attention.

City officials in Casper, however, didn't have the luxury of ignoring the planned protests. With thousands of mourners and hundreds of journalists from around the country about to descend on the town for the memorial service, they had to take every precaution to make sure Phelps—or any other publicity seekers for that matter—created as little a stir as possible. On the night before the memorial service, the city council held a special session and voted unanimously to ban any demonstrations on public property within fifty feet of the service. It wasn't enough to entirely prohibit the Phelps clan from presenting their hateful stage show, but it limited them to a roped-in area in the public park across the street from St. Mark's.

Phelps represented the madness we knew; there was no telling what other trouble the media storm surrounding Matt's murder and memorial service might attract to Casper. In preparation, the police arranged for bomb-sniffing dogs to be stationed outside the church, planned to have a SWAT team in a van across the street from the church, and then, the evening before the memorial service, asked Dennis to wear a bulletproof vest the following morning, when he planned to make a statement to the press.

"A what?" I asked Dennis when he told me the plan. It had been one thing after another that week. But a bulletproof vest? The night before the memorial service, I sat in my hotel room, wondering: How had my family's life come to this? Why was our son's picture in newspapers and on newscasts nationwide? How had our private suffering become such a public spectacle? Why was my husband preparing to wear a bulletproof vest? I tried long and hard that night to answer those questions—but couldn't.

Since that night, I've heard a lot of theories and I've come up with a few of my own. One thought, for example, is that after covering the Monica Lewinsky scandal for months, the press was desperate for something else to report when news of Matt's attack crossed the wires. Matt was light haired and blue eyed, small for his age, and looked like the typical kid next door. For those and countless other reasons, the public immediately identified with him and with our plight as a family. The fact that Matt held on to his precious life for a few days after being found tied to that fence gave people the time to develop an emotional and vested interest in him—to hope, pray, and to hold vigils in support of his recuperation.

Please, don't misunderstand. I was—and continue to be—thankful for every prayer extended in Matt's and our family's direction. But when all that interest ultimately manifested itself in protests outside the memorial service, a guest list and tickets just to make sure my family members and loved ones could get a seat in the sanctuary, a SWAT team, and Dennis in a bulletproof vest, it was overwhelming and scary. I wished with every bit of energy I had left in my body that everyone would just go away—that people would just leave us alone.

THE STORM THAT BLEW into Wyoming on the morning of the memorial service started out with rain, which turned to sleet before transitioning into heavy, wet snow. But it was still raining when Dennis prepared to make his statement to the press in front of city hall. It was to be the first public appearance of a family member since Matt had been attacked. It would attract dozens of reporters—each accompanied by his or her own photographer, cameraman, sound operator, and/or satellite truck. I think people assumed that I wouldn't want anything to do with it. But then, as Dennis got ready, I pulled him aside and asked, "Why am I not going? I'm Matt's mom. I should be there. We should be a family."

I think Dennis was a bit surprised. "Are you sure?" he asked. It wasn't that he doubted that I should, but he didn't think that I wanted to be there. I didn't. I just couldn't imagine not being there, next to him, as he spoke for our family. I needed to be there.

As Dennis and I stood there in the rain, in front of a sea of reporters gathered outside Casper City Hall, I did my best to avoid eye contact with anyone. When Dennis started to speak, my chin began to quiver, and I thought, dammit! The last thing I wanted was to let my emotions to get the better of me. Although most reporters had been respectful of my privacy, I felt that the press, in general, had taken too much from me already. And I didn't want to give them anything else. Nevertheless, my eyes started to well with tears, and suddenly I found myself next to my bulletproof-vested husband without any more protection than his shoulder and my umbrella. Neither was enough to shelter from me from the cameras, whose shutters started going crazy as soon as I began to cry.

"On behalf of our son, we want to thank the citizens of the United States and the people of the world who have expressed their deepest sympathy and condolences to our family during these trying times," Dennis read. "A person as caring and as loving as our son Matt would be overwhelmed by what this incident has done to the hearts and souls of people around the world. Matthew was the type of person that if this would have happened to another person, he would have been first on the scene to offer his help and his heart to the family."

Then he added, "We should try to remember that because Matt's last few minutes of consciousness on Earth might have been hell, his family and friends want more than ever to say their farewells to him in a peaceful, dignified, and loving manner."

Dennis said everything I wanted to and more. Still, the next day the Associated Press reported that, "As he spoke, his wife, Judy, stood weeping behind him, one hand over her mouth."

It was snowing so hard by the time we drove from our hotel to the church that we could barely see out the windows. To be on the safe side, though, the driver made sure to take a route where we wouldn't see the Phelps clan and its virulent protest. The plan, as I understood it, was for us to pull up to the back of the church and then enter through the kitchen, so we could avoid the crowd out front altogether. But somehow, after Dennis and I stepped into the church from the kitchen area, we found ourselves entangled in a line of well-wishers. For what seemed like a half hour or more, we ended up greeting people, comforting them, and thanking them for coming.

Nothing was as it should have been that day, and I woke up knowing that it wouldn't be. Although I was mentally prepared to attend my son's memorial service, the last thing I expected was that we'd actually have to welcome people to the service.

Dennis and I were nearly engulfed by strangers and friends alike. There was really no way we could extricate ourselves. In retrospect, we actually found some comfort in seeing our friends that morning.

Eventually someone came to escort us from the crowd because a representative from the Clinton administration, the secretary of veterans affairs, Togo West, was waiting in another room and wanted to speak with my family before the service. Secretary West was one of two White House representatives there that afternoon. The other was presidential adviser Sean Maloney, who at the time was the highest-ranking openly gay man in the White House. He has since become one of my closest friends. Whenever I was introduced to a public official before, during, or after the memorial service, I felt a rush of anger and asked myself, why does he need to be here? Their sincerity seemed so contrived and staged. I'm sure I hid none of that contempt when I was introduced to Sean. While I don't remember what, if anything, I said to him, I'm sure I was cold, and I've apologized profusely for it in the years since. But Sean promises that I wasn't rude, and I suppose he could have missed my disdain because of the overwhelming despair that also showed on my face.

I think I now have a better understanding of why people like Sean and Secretary West were at the service that afternoon. As much as Dennis, Logan, and I wanted the service to be about the Matt we knew and loved, it was also about

Matthew, the murdered young gay man who millions of people around the world had welcomed into their hearts. What I don't think I fully appreciated at the time was that there were parts of our Matt in their Matthew, and that the millions of people holding vigils around the world and the hundreds of strangers—including Sean Maloney—gathered at St. Mark's that day really were, as much as they could, mourning for the loss of my son.

We were also joined by fifteen of Matt's Switzerland high school friends, and his wonderful adviser. They flew in from all over the world to say good-bye to their Matteo. There were so many of Matt's friends and ours, as well as family, who traveled great distances to be with us that day.

Once I was finally seated in a pew, I was relieved to see that the craziness outside had not affected the serenity inside. As many folks as there were in attendance (every seat in the sanctuary and the adjoining Guild Hall was full, with overflow crowds in two neighboring churches and hundreds more gathered outside), there seemed to be even more flowers. Elton John, who I found out later had tried to contact Dennis and me at the hospital in Fort Collins, had bought out every flower store in town. The church was overflowing with color and the calming, clean fragrance of all those flowers.

People who had been close to Matt—his childhood friend Tim Galles and his godmother—started the service by reading passages from the Bible. His cousin Megan read a poem that she'd composed. Then my niece Anne Kitch Peck, who is an Episcopal priest, gave a very stirring homily.

"Matt was a young man who met the world with eager expectations, who offered trust and friendship easily and lived easily," she said. "Matt trusted in the good of God's world.

"He was not always a winner according to the world's standards," she continued. "He struggled to fit into a world not always kind to gentle spirits. What was important to Matt was to care, to help, to nurture, to bring joy to others in his quiet, gentle way.

"[He] believed that if he made one person's life better, he had succeeded," Anne added. "Judging from the world's response, Matt will have made a difference in the lives of thousands . . . I believe [he] has shown us the way, out of the abyss in which his murder has plunged us. Matt has shown us the way, away from violence, hate, and despair.

"How can we not let our hearts be deeply, deeply troubled?" she asked. "How can we not be immersed in despair? How can we not cry out against this? This is not the way it is supposed to be. A son has died, a brother has been lost, a child has been broken, torn, abandoned. We become engulfed in a turbulent stream of grief, anger, guilt, fear, shame, outrage."

The answer, she said, was in Matt's love for others and in his faith. "Matt is loved by God," she said. "And it is that love that has radiated out of the midst of tragedy, love which empowers his parents to speak in passion rather than condemnation, love which inspired his friends to acts of prayer and witness, love which is more powerful than any voice of hate."

The Reverend Royce W. Brown, of St. Mark's, also offered a eulogy: "There is an image that comes to mind when I reflect on that wooden cross-rail fence," he said. "I replace that image with that of another man hung upon a cross. When I concentrate on that man, I can release the bitterness inside."

He ended with a Bible verse from Romans: "Be not overcome with evil, for evil can be overcome with good."

The verses, the eulogies, the homilies were unbelievably touching. Yet as much as I try, I can't remember a word of them today. I had to rely on the notes of others in order to recount them here. For the previous ten days, I had been constantly reminding myself that what was happening to me and to my family was real—that I wasn't in the middle of a nightmare. But I think I allowed myself to slip into a bit of a dream state that afternoon at the memorial service. As muted light poured through the stained-glass windows, and as the storm outside continued to grow, I simply drank everything in while watching the falling snow cast a cascade of shadows throughout the sanctuary. My heart was warmed to see so many loved ones at the pulpit. But I can't remember a word they said.

I do, however, remember the songs. Led by the chorus in their red robes, we first sang "Amazing Grace" (which I understand the crowd outside also sang, in an effort to drown out the antigay chants from the Phelps crowd) and then opened our hymnals to Eleanor Farjeon's song "Morning Has Broken."

Morning has broken, like the first morning
Praise with elation, God's recreation of the new day

Cat Stevens's version of the song had been among Matt's favorites. Its inclusion in the service was the only request Dennis and I made. Singing it in the sanctuary that afternoon provided me one of very few moments of clarity and hope I'd felt in nearly two weeks. Later, as Bishop Bruce Campbell gave communion, I took a second to note how simple, dignified, and beautiful the service was.

Another moment of clarity was much darker, however: as people passed by Matt's ashes while they were taking communion, I regretted—if only for a fleeting second—that we'd had him cremated. I thought, we should have had an open casket so people could see what those men did to him. I was still under the impression that the majority of the people at the service weren't there for the right reasons. I thought that, just like the reporters that morning, they'd come to Matt's memorial service for the spectacle. I wanted them to truly see what had happened to our son and to figure out why it happened, so they could make sure it never happened again.

As strong as it was, that resentment only lasted a second before it was washed away by the beauty of the service and the deep sincerity of all the words spoken from the pulpit that afternoon. I've occasionally regretted that we didn't allow CNN to broadcast the memorial service from the church that day. As crass as the request seemed at the time, if we'd said okay, I would have a videotape of the service today and could better remember everything that took place—everything everybody said about Matt that afternoon. But then I realize that if such a videotape existed, I might not have been able to leave that moment in time. I might not have been able to move forward.

Thirteen

THE COLDEST PART of the year in Wyoming coincided with the loneliest months in my life—the four months between Matt's memorial service and the beginning of the jury-selection process for the trial of Russell Henderson, the first of the killers to be tried.

It was clear, even when we were still in the hospital with Matt, that one of us would have to stay in Wyoming once the initial madness had subsided—if only to assist prosecutors with their preparation for the trials against Russell Henderson and Aaron McKinney. Since Logan had to get back to school in Minnesota and Dennis needed to return to his job in Saudi Arabia, I was the one left to stick around. Of course, staying behind in Casper and living alone in a hotel room (or crashing with a friend when I could) was the last thing I wanted to do. I desperately wanted to be with my family. After the trauma we'd been through, I knew it would have done us all good to be together. But, in addition to wanting to be nearby so we could help the prosecutors, Dennis and I decided that we should take advantage of the narrow window of time when people were still interested in Matt to see if something, anything positive might be gained from his death. At the time, we weren't sure what we could do, or even what we wanted to do, but it was pretty obvious that whatever we decided probably wouldn't be something we could do from Saudi Arabia.

So, as the wind swept away the snow that had fallen on the day of Matt's memorial service, coating the highways with black ice and ushering in months of subfreezing temperatures, I settled in at a hotel in Casper, for God knows how long.

Dennis wasn't able to return to Saudi Arabia as quickly as we first thought. As fate would have it, we had two more memorial services to attend. The first was for Dennis's eighty-one-year-old uncle. I'd never met him, but he and his wife drove up from Cheyenne to attend Matt's service. The drive takes only about two and a half hours on a good day, but it probably took twice that amount of time in a storm like we had that morning. A history of heart disease and a difficult drive in bad weather was apparently too much for Dennis's uncle. He had a heart attack and died in the church's kitchen as he was on his way into the service. Dennis and I weren't told of his death until after the service was over. We attended his services in Cheyenne three days after Matt's.

Then, three weeks after Matt's memorial service, Dennis's dad, Harry Shepard, passed away. He and his wife, Ruth, left

Wyoming a few days after Matt's service. When they got home to Arizona, Harry started to feel ill—complaining of chills, a fever, and exhaustion. Harry was taken to the hospital. The man who had taught Matt and Logan to hunt, fish, camp, ride horses, and love the outdoors slipped into a coma soon after that. A few hours after that he died from what we later learned was undiagnosed leukemia. There's little question that his illness was exacerbated by the stress we all had to endure after Matt was attacked. All the commotion with the media, being in the hospital room with Matt when he died, the memorial service and protesters, the funeral in Cheyenne, helping us clean out Matt's apartment in Laramie, the long hours without sleep, and the drive back to Arizona were apparently too much, even for a man like him.

The first few months I was back living in Wyoming by myself definitely weren't action packed. The Albany County prosecutor, Cal Rerucha, didn't need a whole lot from me as he prepared for the cases against Henderson and McKinney, but we still did our best to stay in constant contact with each other so I always knew how things were progressing.

Also I wasn't really in touch with many of my old friends from when we lived in Casper, prior to the move to Saudi Arabia. I think no one really knew how to respond to what happened. To be fair, I don't know if I would have known how to act around one of my friends if the tables were turned. I'd gone from being a mother of two sons to being a mother of one struggling to make sense of a murder that made no sense. What do you say to someone like that?

In the many hours I had to myself, I tried to focus on the best possible way that the three of us could honor Matt's memory. Along with the tens of thousands of cards, letters, and e-mails people had sent us since Matt had been attacked, they'd included nearly ninety thousand dollars in donations— much of it in five- and ten-dollar bills and checks from college students—intended to help us out with hospital bills. Fortunately we didn't need people's help to pay for Matt's medical expenses. Instead we decided to use their very gracious gifts to help ensure that Matt's legacy was bigger than his murder and that his story continued long after the world's journalists had turned their attention elsewhere.

On December 1, 1998, on what would have been Matt's twenty-second birthday, his father, brother, and I started the Matthew Shepard Foundation. Our vision for the organization wasn't yet quite clear; though we knew that we wanted it to focus on young people and that we wanted it to be part philanthropic and part educational. We had nevertheless taken the first step toward defining what would be our family's focus for years to come.

DENNIS AND I had known of prosecutor Cal Rerucha from the days when we were all students together at the university. Cal was student-body president back then, and I remember seeing his campaign posters around campus and thinking, "What a strange name." Since graduating, we'd heard Cal's name often—he had a reputation throughout Wyoming as a demanding, tough, and successful prosecutor. But we had never actually met each other until October 1998, when Dennis and I went to the Laramie Police Department for the first time after Matt's death.

After the briefing, Cal took Dennis and me aside and said, "I need to know now if you have any strong feelings about the death penalty. Because if I ask for the death penalty [which the law said was an option in Henderson's and McKinney's cases] and if you come out in public in opposition to it, then that will be a waste of all our time. So I need to know how you feel about it before we get started."

Dennis and I definitely had opinions about the death penalty, and we'd had a chance to discuss them with the boys when the four of us were together in August that summer. It was just a couple of months after James Byrd Jr. had been murdered in Jasper, Texas. What a horrific story that was. Byrd was a forty-nine-year-old African American man who had been grabbed off the street by three white men, who beat him behind a convenience store, chained him by the ankles to the back of their pickup, and then dragged him down a paved road for three miles.

That summer the four of us had discussed how there were instances, as in the Byrd case, where the death penalty was the only just and fair sentence. There was no question that the three suspects were guilty of killing James Byrd. There was also little doubt that if the perpetrators were introduced into the general prison population they would just teach thousands of other men to hate the same way they did. We all agreed that they deserved the death penalty, although as it turned out, only two of the three suspects were sentenced to death. The third was sentenced to life in prison.

We also talked about how, when dealing with a death-penalty case, it was imperative that the court ensured that no stone was left unturned. We'd all heard of instances where people had been sentenced to death and then, afterward, other evidence came to the surface that showed that the suspect should not have been found guilty—and certainly shouldn't have been sentenced to death.

So we all understood that it takes a tremendous leap of faith to state that you're in support of the death penalty—and that it's probably impossible to have blanket support for the issue. Still, as I said, we agreed that there were cases, like the James Byrd murder, where there was no question the suspects were guilty and the death penalty seemed like the only reasonable sentence.

There was never any doubt in anyone's mind that Henderson and McKinney were guilty of killing Matt; yet we also didn't think it was our place to try to determine their sentences or to sway the juries. That was the judge's, jury's, and the prosecution team's job. So when Cal asked us that afternoon how we felt about the death penalty, we chose not to tell him how we felt. "We have opinions that we won't share with you or anyone else," Dennis told him. "We know that you have a job to do, and we'll support whatever decision you make."

So the prospect of the death sentence hung over the Albany County Courthouse on March 24, 1999, when the jury-selection process started for Russell Henderson's trial, but it was probably the furthest thing from my mind that morning. I'd waited nearly five months for the proceeding to get under-way. At that point I was incredibly hopeful that the trial would help answer some of the questions that had been on my mind since October. Primarily, why Matt?

Yet as I entered the courtroom, I was worried about hav-ing to come face-to-face with one of my son's killers, espe-cially since I had to do it on my own because Dennis couldn't leave Saudi Arabia until it was time for the actual trial. I was also anxious about being able to control my emotions. Cal had instructed that it was critical for me to keep my cool so that the defense could never contend that an outburst from me influenced a juror. That would have given them grounds for appeal.

If you didn't count the seventy-plus potential jurors, the courtroom was relatively empty that first morning—surprisingly so given how much media attention had picked up again in anticipation of the trial. Worried that journalists might disrupt his court, Judge Jeffrey Donnell had banned cameras and radio microphones from the courtroom.

I sat in the back of the room—I'm not even certain any of the potential jurors knew who I was—and held my breath when Henderson entered, taking a seat in the front, next to his attorney, public defender Wyatt Skaggs. Dressed in slacks, a button-down shirt, and tie, Henderson looked different—a lot more presentable than he had when he appeared on national newscasts at his arraignment back in October, wearing a prison-issued orange jumpsuit. He'd also grown his hair out a bit—probably on the advice of his attorney—so that he looked a little less intimidating.

Although I'd seen pictures of Henderson in the newspapers and on the TV news, this was the first time I'd laid eyes on him in person. When he finally walked into the room, I was surprised by how little emotion I actually felt toward him. I think it was more indifference than it was numbness, which again surprised me. If I had any feeling at all, it was pity because I knew that he'd had a troubled childhood, which we had been reminded of just months before when his mother was found mysteriously dead along a snowy rural road north of Laramie. I also didn't believe that Henderson had ever intended things to end up the way they did; he was deathly afraid of McKinney and apparently did everything that his friend ordered. I also felt pity because, as he walked into the courtroom that day, he seemed to show some remorse. Today I'm not so certain that the remorse Henderson showed was genuine. It's more likely that I projected it onto him, or, at best, the remorse was a reflection of his deep regret that he'd put himself in a life-or-death situation and not because of what he'd done to Matt.

The courtroom setup reminded me of a church, with the potential jurors sitting in what might have otherwise been the pews. Henderson and the prosecution and defense teams sat at tables toward the front. As the lawyers addressed the room, defense attorney Skaggs turned Henderson so that he faced the potential jurors. At one point, Henderson's and my eyes locked. I wasn't sure that he knew who I was, but that didn't matter; my body flooded with adrenaline, my heart nearly leapt out of my chest, and I did whatever I could to make sure that it never happened again. Luckily, it didn't.

Cal and Wyatt Skaggs made certain that potential jurors knew what trial they were being considered for. Skaggs even told them that Henderson, who was charged with first-degree murder, kidnapping, and aggravated robbery, would admit that he left the Fireside Lounge with Matt and that he stood by and watched McKinney pistol-whip Matt. But Henderson did not, Skaggs told the jury, join in the beating or the robbery.

"On October 6, he, Henderson, accompanied Aaron McKinney and Matthew Shepard. He drove the pickup, which he knew was owned by McKinney. He was witness to the beating with a pistol owned by McKinney," Skaggs said. "Those are our admissions. They're proven. I give them to you right from the beginning." But the trial, he added, was not about "hate, but more mundane motives such as robbery."

Matt's killing, he said, "has literally injected our community with a feeling of guilt. The press wants us to think that we are somehow responsible for what went on October 6 . . . Are any of you here going to judge this case because you feel guilty and want to make a statement to the nation?

"This case is not about hate," Skaggs continued. "All crimes . . . aren't about hate. They come down to some real simple motives." Then, putting his hand on Henderson's shoulder, he did his best to make Henderson a sympathetic figure in the potential jurors' eyes: "This Russell Henderson is a twenty-one-year-old who's lived here all his life. He's not a defendant. He's a living, breathing human being . . . Are you going to give him a fair shot?"

Cal, for his part, refuted any suggestion that the trial would, in any way, be routine. He told the potential jurors that, if selected, they'd first have to live up to an incredibly important constitutional responsibility.

"Whether black or white, rich or poor, Catholic or Protestant or even atheist, whether we have power or no power, whether we are straight or whether we are gay, we are equal because the Wyoming constitution tells us we are equal," he said. "If any of you cannot follow that element of the constitution, you cannot sit on this jury."

He also made it clear that the prospective jurors, if selected, would be subjected to the details of a violent murder, including graphic and disturbing photographs of the crime scene and of Matt's injuries. In addition, Cal said, they wouldn't only be asked to determine if Henderson was guilty; if they found him guilty, they'd also have to decide whether he deserved to live or die.

"It is not a duty that can be performed through the tears of pity, and it is not a duty that can be performed when the fire of rage burns in your belly and you judge through those eyes," Cal said.

Opening arguments in Henderson's trial were set to begin Monday, April 5, 1999, the day after Easter. The Thursday before, it appeared that everything was on track for that date: The defense and prosecution teams had narrowed the pool of potential jurors down to forty-seven, and they were prepared to narrow the group down again, to the final twelve plus alternates. But then on Good Friday, Cal got a telephone call from Wyatt Skaggs, saying that Henderson wanted to plea-bargain. He was willing to plead guilty, testify against Aaron McKinney, and allocute (essentially, tell his story, admit his guilt) on the stand in exchange for two life sentences, to be served concurrently or consecutively, depending on the judge's discretion.

Cal and I talked it over with the prosecution team, but I couldn't do anything without conferring with Dennis. And once I did, it was clear that we all agreed that the deal made sense. Based on everything the police and the prosecutors told us, Dennis and I believed Henderson when he said he never hit Matt (although he did follow McKinney's order and tie Matt to the fence, which in the eyes of the law made him as guilty as McKinney because he did nothing to stop him from beating Matt). We also agreed that the jury was likely to condemn Henderson to the maximum sentence allowed without the death penalty, even though he was technically eligible for the death sentence. By agreeing to the deal, Dennis and I realized that we could assure Henderson would get the maximum sentence and that we wouldn't have to go through the difficulty of the trial or the frustration and pain of endless appeals. That in itself would be a huge relief. In addition, Albany County officials were predicting that the cost of the trial might eat up a full 10 percent of the county's budget, resulting in the slashing of funding for social service agencies by as much as $100,000. At that time, there was no recourse for federal assistance because there was no federal hate crime law that included sexual orientation. Therefore, the county could not expect to receive any federal funds to offset the costs of the trial.

By agreeing to the deal that Henderson and his defense team proposed, Dennis and I could save our family from additional pain, prevent the county from cutbacks, and ensure that justice was served. So we did just that, and then Dennis rushed to Laramie from Saudi Arabia to make sure he would be there on Monday, April 5, for what would now be Russell Henderson's sentencing, rather than the start of his trial.

I wasn't surprised when I heard that Fred Phelps and the clan from his Westboro Baptist Church planned to picket outside the courthouse that Monday. The group had gained so much notoriety after demonstrating outside the memorial service that they'd begun to exploit anything and everything to do with Matt, incorporating posters with his image and the slogan "Matthew in Hell" right along with the "God Hates Fags," "God Hates You," and "Fag Sin" posters that they brandished during their antigay demonstrations across the country.

Just as Casper city officials had done in October, Laramie officials did everything they could to ensure that Phelps wouldn't disrupt the proceeding: A court order restricted all protests to an area on the west side of the courthouse, where they wouldn't interfere with the business at hand. And there was added protection from Phelps this time around. Romaine Patterson (the friend Matt met in Casper and followed to Denver), her friends, and others came up with one of the most amazing responses, which the group called Angel Action. It involved using white sheets and PVC pipe to create angel costumes with giant wings. Wearing the costumes, the angels marched up to the Albany County Courthouse and encircled the Westboro Baptist Church protestors, blocking their view and making sure that nobody had to see their hateful signs.

As the group surrounded Phelps, Romaine read a statement:

Before you stands a band of angels. We come from a number of backgrounds: We don't represent any one group; any one religion, sex, race, age, or sexual orientation. They are merely a group of people who joined with me because they believe in honesty and truth. So often we find that people are willing to make a lot of noise about what they believe to be true. We don't believe that we have to say anything at all. Aside from this brief explanatory statement our actions will speak for themselves. Just one look and the truth is plainly clear. Our focus is to bring forth a message of peace and love. Hatred is running rampant through our everyday lives. But as a group, we choose to lift ourselves above that hatred. We feel, as so many others do, that love and compassion for our community and our humanity are the answers that so many people are desperately searching for.

And so we bring forth a message—from God, if you will:

Love, respect, and compassion for everyone is why we are here today. I could no longer sit idly by and watch others bring forth messages that were nothing more than vindictive and hate filled. As a young person, I feel it necessary to show the great nation that we live in that there doesn't need to be this kind of violence and hatred in our world. And that loving one another doesn't mean that we have to compromise our beliefs; it simply means that we choose to be compassionate and respectful of others.

Dennis and I didn't see Romaine and her angels that day, since we came into the courthouse through the underground garage in the back of the building, but we were incredibly touched by their compassion and creativity. More important, their work has inspired thousands of other people around the country, who download the do-it-yourself angel kit online and launch their own Angel Action whenever the Phelps clan comes to town, whether it's to protest a gay and lesbian pride parade or a soldier's funeral.

I SPENT THE NIGHT prior to Henderson's sentencing preparing a victim's impact statement to read to the court. There was so much I wanted to say—about our family's love for Matt; about the passion, curiosity, and empathy that defined his too-short life; and about how his murder left an irreversible void in his brother's, his father's, and my hearts. Before I sat down to write, I couldn't imagine how I would put all my thoughts and feelings onto paper. But once I started to write, the words flowed like water, probably because they'd been dammed in my head and heart for so long. As the hearing began on Monday morning, I summoned all the courage I could and walked to the podium at the front of the courtroom and spoke my heart:

"I want to thank the court for this opportunity to talk about Matt," I began, my voice cracking nearly as soon as I started speaking. "I feel that I must try to share with you what Matt's life and death have meant to us. It is important that he be re-vealed to you as a loving, vibrant, kind young man. You need to see him as we do to try and understand our loss. However, I am not sure we really understand it yet ourselves . . .

"I love [Matt] more than I can express in this statement," I continued. "There aren't enough words to describe how much I love him. We shared so much—late-night talks try-ing to solve the problems of surviving in this world as we saw them, politics, love of good movies and bad, theater, books, good food, and conversation. He was my son, my firstborn and more. He was my friend, my confidant, my constant re-minder of how good life can be—and, ultimately, how hurt-ful. I will never understand why anyone would want to hurt Matt—to act with such cruelty, such disregard for another human being . . ."

I started to cry at this point, but I wasn't really as self-conscious about it as I usually am. In fact, the courtroom was so quiet—and I was so focused on the words in front of me—that I don't think I even gave my tears a second thought. I only remember marveling at how hard my heart was beating.

"What would our lives be like now, without Matt? Logan had planned to attend the University of Wyoming. He and Matt were going to share an apartment—both looking for-ward to the time they would spend together, getting to know each other once again. That hope was killed. All our hopes for

Matt were killed. All the hopes and dreams that were Matt's were killed for twenty dollars and some twisted reason known only to his killers . . .

"How have our lives changed?

"I can't answer that yet. I know personally that there is a hole in my life. I will never experience Matt's laugh, his wonderful hugs, his stories, hear about his ambitions for the future.

"There are days when I think I can't go on. Then I remember Logan and Dennis, our extended families, and our wonderful friends—new and old. I know their love and support will sustain me. I know Matt would be very disappointed in me if I gave up.

"He would be disappointed in us all if we gave up . . ."

My statement couldn't have taken more than ten minutes to read, but it took everything I had in me to do so. When I sat down next to Dennis, I was shaken, flushed, and completely spent. The hearing was far from over, though.

Next Henderson's grandmother, Lucy Thompson, addressed the court:

As the grandmother and the person who has raised Russell, along with my family, we have written the following statement: Our hearts ached for the pain and suffering that the Shepards have gone through. We have prayed for your family since the very beginning. Many times throughout the day I have thought about Matt. You will continue to be in our thoughts and prayers, as we know that your pain will never go away. You have showed such mercy in allowing us to have this plea, and we are so grateful that you are giving us all the opportunity to live. Your Honor, we as a family, hope that, as you sentence Russell, that you will do it concurrently two life terms. For the Russell we know and love, we humbly plead, Your Honor, to not take Russell completely out of our lives forever.

I squeezed Dennis's hand as Mrs. Thompson spoke. As devastated as we were by the loss of our son, we understood that she was, in a very real way, about to lose the grandson she'd raised as her own son. I'm sure she was as baffled by his actions that October night as Dennis, Logan, and I were. As she begged the court for mercy that day, I'm sure she was doing so for the grandson she knew and loved, not the man who killed Matt. I was heartbroken—simply devastated—by her loss. Those two boys, Henderson and McKinney, hadn't only torn my family apart; they'd ruined their own families as well. Henderson's grandmother was a very well-respected woman in Laramie. She owned a day-care center, was a very devout Mormon, and everybody loved her. She didn't deserve to have this happen to her—none of us did. And as she spoke that day, I could see that her heart was breaking, for all our families.

Nevertheless, it was the judge who was deciding Henderson's fate that day. So after Mrs. Thompson returned to her seat, Judge Donnell turned to her grandson. "Mr. Henderson," he said, "you have a constitutional right to make a statement if you would like to do so. Do you have anything you would like to say?"

"Yes, I do, Your Honor," Henderson coughed, as he stood and turned toward Dennis and me. Still holding Dennis's hand, I clenched my jaw and fought every urge I had to look away. I owed it to Matt, I thought, to listen to everything Henderson said as closely as I could. And as much as I wanted to, that meant not looking away.

"Mr. and Mrs. Shepard, there's not a moment that goes by that I don't see what happened that night. I know what I did was very wrong, and I regret greatly what I did. You have my greatest sympathy for what happened. I hope that someday you will be able to find it within your hearts to forgive me. Your Honor, I know what I did was wrong. I'm very sorry for what I did, and I'm ready to pay my debt for what I did."

Despite the remorse I thought I'd seen in Henderson's eyes just a couple weeks before, at the beginning of the jury selection process, his words that afternoon sounded hollow. Did he regret his action or did he regret getting caught? I wondered. His voice was flat, unfeeling, and in no way matched the words coming out of his mouth. Listening to his apology, I couldn't bring myself to believe that he was truly sorry. His statement felt like yet another stage in a months-long shell game. Rather than trying to get Matt to get in the truck with him and McKinney, this time Henderson was desperately attempting to elicit pity from the judge.

But this time his tricks didn't work; Judge Donnell didn't believe Henderson any more than I did. "Mr. Henderson, you drove the vehicle that took Matthew Shepard to his death," he said after Henderson retook his seat. "You bound him to that fence in order that he might be more savagely beaten and in order that he might not escape to tell his tale. You left him out there for eighteen hours, knowing full well that he was there. Perhaps having an opportunity to save his life, and you did nothing. Mr. Henderson, this court does not believe that you really feel any remorse for your part in this matter. And I wonder whether you fully realize the gravity of what you've done.

"The court finds it appropriate, therefore, that sentence be ordered as followed: As to count three, that being felony murder with robbery, you are to serve a term of imprisonment for the term of your natural life. On count one, kidnapping, that you serve a period of imprisonment for the term of your natural life. Sentence for count one to run consecutive to sentencing for count three."

FOR ALL THE BENEFITS that came with Dennis's and my decision to agree to Henderson's plea bargain, there was one giant downside: We didn't get any answers to the questions that had been hounding us since the night of the attack. Most notably, why? Henderson recounted the events of the night of October 6 and the early morning of October 7, and he even disclosed how he and McKinney (together with their girlfriends, Pasley and Price respectively) conspired to cover up the truth and attempted to get rid of the evidence—going so far as to hide Matt's wallet in one of McKinney's son's dirty diapers. But because the plea bargain and the subsequent sentencing took place before Henderson's actual trial ever got underway, Cal never got to ask Henderson—or any witnesses, for that matter—to expand on any of the details of the case. He never got a chance to ask why. Even though justice had been served, I was left wondering.

Henderson's aborted trial left the press a little unfulfilled, too. There's nothing a journalist likes more than a good story (except for maybe beating everybody else to that story), and Henderson's plea bargain not only left a lot of questions unanswered, it left a lot of column inches empty.

That, combined with the coincidence that jury selection for McKinney's trial commenced October 11, almost exactly one year to the day after Matt died, resulted in an even bigger media circus than we'd seen at the start of the Henderson proceeding. On Sunday night, the night before jury selection started, more than six hundred people gathered in Laramie for a candlelight vigil in Matt's honor, which was followed by a Peter, Paul and Mary tribute concert on the University of Wyoming campus. Before the concert, Peter Yarrow told the press that "Peter, Paul and Mary came to Laramie to embrace the people of Laramie, the students, and to dignify and acknowledge the death of Matthew Shepard." He took pains to point out that hatred wasn't an inherent part of Laramie: "There are hundreds of Hendersons and McKinneys and thousands and thousands of Matthew Shepards," he said. "Part of us died with him." Peter also told those gathered at the vigil that he'd taken a trip out to the rough-hewn fence where Matt had been left to die a year before. "I knelt down and I wept," he said. "We will not forget him."

When Yarrow got to the fence, he probably saw 150 teddy bears left there by two young men, who had hiked the eighty-mile journey from Fort Collins to Laramie and back again to bring the bears (each of which represented a different hate-crime victim) and leave them at the fence.

Further—and less welcome—commotion was created by some Catholic organizations. The groups bought a series of two-page ads in newspapers across Wyoming, campaigning against the death penalty in McKinney's case. Dennis and I were both very offended by this campaign. In our minds, not only did it violate the incredibly sacred separation between church and state, but it threatened to compromise the jury pools. The continued media frenzy around Matt's attack had already made certain that selecting a jury would be difficult, and it seemed inexcusable that the Catholic Church, or any church, could get away with pushing its doctrine on potential jurors. Since then, Dennis and I have often wondered how the church could get away with those ads without putting its tax-exempt status at risk.

BEFORE MATT DIED, I'd heard lots of people discuss how difficult the anniversary of a loved one's death could be. I always discounted this talk—even after I'd lost my son. It was just a day, I thought. What difference could a day make in the severity of a person's mourning? For better or worse, I'd pretty successfully kept a cap on my emotions during the months following Matt's death. But then came October. I was bowled over by grief, and there seemed to be no escaping it. October 6 screamed, "This is the day Matt was attacked!" And October 12 yelled, "Today's the day you lost your precious son!" Suddenly I understood the pain people had always described, and I've been reminded of it every October since. I hate October.

So that October 11, the day before the anniversary of Matt's passing, satellite trucks clogged the streets in front of the three stories of sandstone that make up the Albany County Courthouse. Fred Phelps and his clan of protestors hoisted their homophobic signs as Angel Action put its wings into action again. And the press clamored for Dennis's and my attention as we made our way into the courtroom. I was surprisingly comforted by the chaos. At the very least, it gave me something else to think about other than what had happened a year earlier.

As it turned out, Dennis and I missed most of the craziness outside the courthouse because, as had been the case during the Henderson proceeding, we were always ushered in and out of the building through the underground garage. This measure was intended to protect us, but it did quite the opposite near the end of the trial, when schedules must have been crossed and we came face-to-face with our son's killer.

Of course we'd both seen McKinney before—I'd sat behind him every day in the courtroom since the first day of jury selection. But in that setting we were protected by protocol and the simple fact that we knew he'd be there. Aaron McKinney was the man on trial, so no element of shock or surprise came with seeing him in court each day.

It caught us completely off guard that morning in the basement hallway that led from the underground garage to the courtroom. Dennis and I were being ushered into the building—and into the elevator corridor—just as McKinney was coming out of the elevator. We weren't at all emotionally prepared to come face-to-face with McKinney like that. When we did, it took my breath away. I'd venture to say that McKinney was as stunned to see us as we were to see him. The three of us stood there, staring at each other, Dennis and I frozen in place and McKinney bound by shackles at his wrists and midsection.

As he had every day since the start of jury selection,

McKinney was wearing an ill-fitting suit. Before, I'd always thought the suits made him resemble his nickname, Dopey. He looked almost sympathetic, like he was too young to have grown-up clothes and had to make do with hand-me-downs. But that morning there were none of the intentional or unintentional theatrics that you find in the courtroom, and there was no illusion of innocence. As we stared each other down, I thought, there's a guilty man. He'd already confessed to killing Matt, and I'd never had any reason to doubt his confession. But it wasn't until I'd come face-to-face with him and had the chance to look into his dark and empty eyes, that I fully understood just how guilty he was.

The encounter must have only lasted fifteen seconds, tops, before the victims-rights advocate who was escorting us yelled, "Get him out of here!" and McKinney was shuffled out of our sight.

THERE SEEMED TO BE fewer surprises during the actual trial itself. Perhaps this was because I'd had an entire year to imagine how the proceeding might play out, and in that time I'd grown pretty good at imagining and expecting the worst. It was also helpful that both the prosecution and defense teams were very clear at the beginning, outlining their game plans. As much as Judge Barton Voigt allowed them to, the lawyers pretty much stuck to what they had proposed.

Cal started by simply laying out the facts of the case, describing how Matt met McKinney and Henderson at the Fireside Lounge. He used specifics from Henderson's and McKinney's earlier confessions and interviews with the police to detail how my son's murderers pretended to be gay in order to lure Matt into McKinney's truck, how McKinney demanded Matt's wallet and then started beating him after finding only twenty dollars, and how, upon reaching the split-rail fence on the east end of town, Henderson followed McKinney's orders and tied Matt to the fence—making it impossible for Matt to defend himself from McKinney's final blows to his head with the butt of his .357 Magnum.

Cal then recounted how Henderson and McKinney, possibly on their way to steal more money from what they thought was Matt's apartment, got into the scuffle with vandals Jeremy Herrera and Emiliano Morales and how, when police officers responded to reports of Herrera's and Morales's delinquency, they stumbled upon McKinney and Henderson and subsequently found the bloodied pistol, bloodstained clothes, and a bank card with Matt's name on it.

Nearly eighteen hours later, Cal continued to explain how, after college student Aaron Kreifels crashed his mountain bike and found the comatose Matt still tied to the fence, police investigators were able to connect the evidence from the truck with the young man who had to be rushed to the hospital in Fort Collins. When Matt died four days later, the police were able to charge McKinney and Henderson with murder. The autopsy report and forensic tests conducted on the evidence from the truck and on Matt's, Henderson's, and McKinney's clothes (some of which the suspects had tried to hide in a truck-stop dumpster outside Cheyenne) only confirmed everything they suspected.

"At the conclusion of the evidence, ladies and gentlemen, the evidence will be overwhelming for kidnapping, for robbery and for aggravated robbery, and for premeditated first-degree murder with malice," Cal said to the jury members. "I will ask for your consideration, and we will ask for your guilty verdicts on all three counts."

Like he'd done before, in what we thought would be Henderson's trial, Cal instructed me to keep as low a profile as possible during the proceeding. Any crying on my part, he said, would give the defense ammunition to seek a mistrial, suggesting that my show of emotion influenced the jury. Just as I'd done for the previous twelve months, I was pretty successful at keeping a cap on my feelings—even when they played McKinney's taped confession, where he described, blow by blow, how he killed Matt. Again, it wasn't that hearing these details didn't tear me apart. Of course it did. But I tried to keep my mind focused on the ultimate goal—justice and the conviction of my son's killer.

While I sat in the courtroom, I did my best to separate myself from the testimony. I didn't go so far as to pretend that they were talking about someone other than Matt, but I tried to process everything I was hearing in as clinical a manner as I could.

My method worked for the most part, until Matt's clothes— a tan, checkered shirt and chinos—were entered into evidence. I think I'd been able to disassociate from the other details of the murder partly because nothing that happened that night had anything to do with my own memories of Matt. But the clothing was a different story. I'd seen him wearing the same shirt and pants many times before, as recently as a month before he was killed. I didn't pay much attention to his outfit back then, though—not any more than I imagine anybody gives someone else's clothes. They were clean and respectable and they fit, and as his mother, that's all that really mattered to me at the time.

But when Matt's shirt and pants were presented to the jury, his clothes took on a much more powerful meaning. In my head, at least, it was a very personal extension of him as the young man I remembered, not the man whom I'd heard referred to in clinical terms by the doctors, investigators, and pathologists who'd been taking the stand. Seeing Matt's clothes bloodied and pinned flat against a presentation board made it impossible for me to intellectualize the testimony that was being offered that day. That was Matt's blood on Matt's clothes. The holes in both his shirt and pants weren't there because Matt had worn them out but were left from the samples that FBI agents had cut out for biological testing. I was there because my son had been murdered—plain and simple. In that moment there was a crack in my composure, and I had to bite my lip to keep from crying.

Worse yet, though, was the day that a doctor took the stand to testify to Matt's level of consciousness during the eighteen hours that he was tied to the fence.

Ever since hearing the horrific details of Matt's murder, knowing that he couldn't feel pain—that he didn't suffer during that long October day and night—comforted me most. So it shook me to the core when the witness suggested that everything Dennis and I had been told in the hospital about Matt's inability to feel pain might not be true. I'm not sure if I gasped, or what I did to attract everyone's attention. But suddenly it seemed like every pair of eyes in the room was pointed in my direction and waiting to see how I was responding to what the doctor was saying. I needed to cry and I could tell, by the flushing of my face and the quickening of my pulse, that I was about to. But I'd gotten so good at the mind-over-matter thing that I just stared at the floor, keeping my emotions at bay until the court recessed and I could race to the ladies' room.

Just as Cal did, the defense team laid out its strategy—as reprehensible as it was—in its opening statement. McKinney's attorneys, Dion Custis and Jason Tangeman, didn't deny that their client had killed Matt but instead contended that the murder wasn't premeditated and was actually provoked by drug use and repressed memories of prior sexual molestation. Apparently those feelings were triggered by what they suggested were unprovoked come-ons from Matt.

"[McKinney] did not intend to cause the death of Matthew Shepard," Tangeman told the jury. "Matthew Shepard did not die during the unbroken chain of events of a robbery. The defense in this case will argue that Matthew Shepard died during five minutes of emotional rage and chaos. The defense will argue that Matthew Shepard died as a result of the heat of passion. Matthew Shepard died because Aaron McKinney lost control of his emotions, and he became, in his words, furious."

McKinney, Tangeman maintained, was addicted to crystal methamphetamine and was smoking or snorting as much as two grams of the drug every week. The drug, he told the jury, is made from common household products and has been known to cause hyperactive behavior, paranoia, sleeplessness, and weight loss. McKinney and Henderson, he said, had been on a three-day bender starting September 26, when McKinney bought Henderson an eighth of an ounce of the drug for his birthday. "During the next week, Aaron and Russell were a little burned out, but Aaron does a little more meth to get him through the week," Tangeman said.

By bringing this up, Tangeman was suggesting to the jury that McKinney wasn't of sound mind on the night of October 6, that he couldn't be held responsible for his own decisions— or that he couldn't even make his own decisions—because he'd spent the better part of the previous two weeks high.

I didn't have any doubt that McKinney was a drug user or even an addict. According to state statistics, as many as 12.6 percent of Wyoming high school students admitted to using crystal in 1999. And while neither McKinney nor Henderson were high school students (actually, they were high school dropouts), it wouldn't surprise me that they would have gotten caught up in that scene. What I took issue with, though, was the suggestion that McKinney's drug use—or even his drug addiction—somehow meant that he wasn't responsible for his actions or that he was somehow incapable of controlling himself. I know that crystal meth can prompt people to do a lot of stupid things—not the least of which is to continue to take the drug. But nowhere have I read that it causes users to kill or that it overrides a person's ability to make conscious and deliberate choices. McKinney could have planned to kill Matt just as easily as he and Henderson planned to pay for pitchers of beer with spare change before heading to the Fireside that night.

Before the trial got underway, Cal had warned Dennis and me that McKinney's attorneys might try to use a controversial "gay panic" argument, which was a defense that alleges that a suspect in a murder case was rendered violently and temporarily insane as a result of same-sex sexual advances.

I'd heard about "gay panic" before, most notably in what had been known as the *Jenny Jones* murder in 1995. In that case, a young man named Jonathan Schmitz killed his friend Scott Amedure after Amedure, who was gay, revealed his crush on Schmitz, who was straight, on the *Jenny Jones Show*. Schmitz didn't deny that he killed Amedure but said that Amedure's advance embarrassed and humiliated him so much that he was unable to control his decision to kill him.

I'd also heard that "gay panic" was seldom successful as a defense. In the *Jenny Jones* case, for example, the judge determined that, because Schmitz waited three days between the taping of the show and killing Amedure, the murder was premeditated and, therefore, couldn't be the result of so-called gay panic. Still, I worried that any attempt to use this defense in McKinney's trial would involve dragging Matt's name through the mud.

Neither Tangeman nor Custis ever used the words "gay panic" in their argument, but it was immediately clear that that was what they were angling for when Tangeman, in his opening argument, told the jury that their client had been molested as a child:

"Aaron McKinney has some sexually traumatic and confusing events in his life," Tangeman said. "Ironically, Aaron McKinney grew up in Imperial Heights, a subdivision right outside of where Matthew Shepard was beaten. And when Aaron was growing up there was a neighborhood bully three or four years older than Aaron. This neighborhood bully was abusing children in Imperial Heights. At age seven, Aaron was forced to suck the penis of the neighborhood bully. At age seven, Aaron was forced to commit sexual acts with another little boy. As a little boy growing up, this bully would tell other neighborhood children that Aaron was a homosexual and that he engaged in homosexual acts, which Aaron will tell you this humiliated him.

"The question will be, did Aaron carry this with him fifteen years later? And at fifteen Aaron's confusing, sexually traumatic past was still with him. He engaged in homosexual sex one time with his cousin.

"But [at] age twenty, just a year before he met Matthew Shepard, he is in Florida with his fiancée-girlfriend Kristen," Tangeman continued. "They go to a church; they go to a gay and lesbian church. He goes inside and sits with Kristen, and he sees men holding hands and kissing, and he turned to Kristen and says, 'We got to get out of here. I have got to go,' and they go outside the church and Kristen finds him sobbing outside."

Just as I had feared, it wasn't enough for the defense team to try to make the jury feel sorry for McKinney; they had to turn its attention to Matt—to allege that he, by coming on to McKinney, triggered the same emotions that caused McKinney to run out of that Florida church. Mind you, however, McKinney didn't kill any of those parishioners.

"The evidence is going to show that it is the advance of Mr. Shepard—the homosexual advance of Mr. Shepard—that was significant to Aaron McKinney," Tangeman said. "That humiliated him in front of his friend Russell Henderson. His past bubbled up in him. He was fueled by drugs. He was fueled by alcohol. And in his own words, he left his body."

McKinney didn't testify in his own defense. Instead jurors heard his taped confession to police, in which he alleged that, while the three of them were in the truck, Matt flirted with him. In an attempt to substantiate these claims McKinney's attorneys called two witnesses to the stand.

The first of the two, the bartender who had beaten up Matt in Cody, was allowed to do something I'd never heard before: testify by phone. I guess I wasn't surprised by what the bartender had to say, mostly because I'd already read it in the papers; he told the jurors that he'd hit Matt that night by the lake because Matt had made a pass at him and hadn't taken no for an answer. I didn't believe the bartender that day in court any more than I did when I read what he had to say in the news. To me, that the bartender didn't actually come to Laramie to testify in person made his side of the story even less believable.

The defense's next witness was a young man who had been at the Fireside that night and who told the court that Matt had tried to pick him up before leaving the bar. According to his testimony, he was sitting by himself at a table when Matt came over, sat down, and introduced himself.

"He sat with me," the man said. "I began to feel really uncomfortable. I didn't like his presence, I guess. I don't know."

When Custis asked why he felt uncomfortable, he replied: "Because of the things I was thinking in my head, I guess. [Matt's] motives for sitting with me."

According to the witness, Matt tried to make conversation until Henderson came over and said something to Matt, and then the two of them walked away.

"Matthew kind of gathered up his stuff—he had cigarettes, lighter, his beer—and he—he just started to take off back to wherever he had come from," the man told the court. "And that is when Matthew kind of stood up and said to me in a sexy voice—I can't explain to you exactly what it was like, but he said he would be back. So I said, 'What?' He leaned down and said something about head, which at the time was really offensive to me. There were a lot of other words, but 'head,' that is the only one I actually caught. And in there he also licked his lips—I believe it wasn't a my-lips-are-chapped kind of lick; it was him trying to be sexy. I believe it was him showing he was interested in me, hitting on me. Then he took off, but I think he got the idea that I was really mad when he did that."

Then, trying to prove that his client wasn't the only one suffering from "gay panic" that night at the Fireside, Custis said to the man, "And during the whole time [Matt] was sitting with you, and then he left you, you said that at some point you did get angry."

To which the witness responded, "When he stood up and gave me the sexy voice and licked his lips, yeah, it set off something inside of me that made me really angry to a certain extent. I mean, it was anger that I wouldn't have wanted to follow through with, but it was anger."

I was steaming at this point. Not so much because of what had been said. I think the bar patron's testimony was more a reflection of his ignorance about gay people than it was about anything Matt said or did. He, rightfully, assumed that night that Matt was gay and, when Matt came up to talk with him, let his ignorance scare him into assuming that Matt was after him. No, what really infuriated me was how McKinney's defense team exploited the witness's naïveté in their effort to paint Matt as a predator. If you look back at his testimony, you see that Matt did nothing more than introduce himself, try to make conversation, lick his lips, say he'd be back, and utter what sounded like the word "head." From what I could tell, it was the bar patron's fear-fueled imagination that added the sexual context to everything Matt said. Even though Cal objected to the defense's leading questions, the judge allowed them to proceed. Custis's questions were clearly attempting to steer the jury into believing that a gay man could send a straight man—or even two straight men—into a murderous fury simply by flirting.

That, at its core, is what's wrong with the gay panic defense Tangeman and Custis were trying to use. None of the allegations that were made against Matt were justification for murder. The witness from the Fireside could have asked Matt to leave and could have cussed him out if he refused to do so. McKinney could have shoved Matt's hand away. He could have ordered Henderson to stop the truck and then kicked Matt out. I don't believe anything that the Cody bartender, the bar patron, or McKinney says Matt did. But even if my son had done all of it, it wouldn't have justified killing. It wouldn't have justified McKinney's decision to hit Matt again and again and again with the butt of a pistol. If making an unwarranted pass were a good excuse for killing someone, there would be a lot more straight men out there getting murdered.

Judge Voigt was as offended by the gay panic defense as Dennis and I were. He suggested as much from the outset—right after Tangeman's opening argument. "I'm concerned about this and where it's going," he told the attorneys. "We [in Wyoming] do not have a gay panic defense, and I don't know if I'm going to allow it." Ultimately, the judge decided against allowing the tactic, saying that it was essentially the same as the battered wife and temporary insanity defenses, neither of which were allowed under Wyoming law. "There is no proffered evidence of a homosexual-rage syndrome that would make the evidence relevant," the judge said. "Even if relevant, the evidence will mislead and confuse the jury, specifically because the defense asks the jury to consider provocation and the heat of passion as negating specific intent, rather than malice, which is contrary to the law as it will be explained to the jury."

In ruling against the defense tactic, Voigt ordered the jury to judge McKinney based on his actions rather than what anybody thought was (or wasn't) going on in his head that night. His decision, on Monday, November 1, essentially cut the defense team's argument off at the knees, and the case went to the jury by the end of the following day.

Dennis and I were pretty confident in Cal's case—doubly so after Voigt ruled against the gay panic defense. We had no doubt that McKinney would be found guilty—we just weren't sure what the jury would find him guilty of. Cal asked for first-degree, premeditated murder—based on the fact that there were a series of events leading up to Matt's murder that night, all of which required a decision on McKinney's part and any number of which he could have decided against following through with. But the defense maintained that none of the murder was predetermined and told the jury that McKinney hadn't intended to kill Matt.

Still, Dennis and I didn't know what to make of the news on Wednesday that the jury, after only ten hours of deliberation, had reached a decision. I remember being incredibly nervous when we returned to the courthouse that afternoon and took our seats.

McKinney must have been nervous, too. He stood facing the jury, his arms crossed against his chest, as it prepared to announce its decision. As the first verdict was read—guilty of kidnapping—his hands fell to his side. He showed no other sign of real emotion as the other two verdicts—guilty both of felony murder and second-degree murder—were revealed.

I was terribly disappointed in the verdict at first; I couldn't help but want what I considered the fullest justice. I found out later that the jury had voted eleven to one in favor of premeditated murder, but that lone holdout was enough to allow McKinney to escape a first-degree murder verdict.

McKinney didn't escape consideration for the death penalty, though; the kidnapping verdict kept that on the table. Just a few hours later, I got a call from Cal saying that Tangeman and Custis wanted to discuss a plea bargain for their client. Essentially, they wanted the same deal Henderson received: McKinney agreed to never appeal and to never talk to the press or profit from the case in exchange for two consecutive life sentences instead of the death penalty.

Just as with Henderson, Dennis and I were of two minds regarding the offer. On one hand, we thought it wasn't our place to make that kind of deal. On the other hand, we thought: You know what? We have a family—we have a younger son—and this would be a way to get McKinney completely out of our lives. We would never have to deal with him again. In addition, it would mean we could avoid the sentencing phase of the trial where there would be fewer restrictions on testimony and McKinney's attorneys could drag Matt's reputation through the mud in order to try to save their client's life.

Meeting with Tangeman and Custis to discuss the deal proved difficult, though. We worried about Dennis attending because of his temper. So I went instead, accompanied by Commander Dave O'Malley and Detective Rob DeBree. It's a good thing that Dennis didn't go. When McKinney's attorneys offered me their sympathies for Matt's death, even I wanted to throw a punch. Intellectually, I knew they were just doing their job, but emotionally I wondered how in the world they could defend a man like McKinney. Just by association, the defense lawyers were as despicable in my mind as he was. Still, after hearing what the lawyers had to say, and after much discussion with Cal and Dennis, we all agreed to the deal.

The following day, before Judge Voigt announced his verdict—which, as with Henderson, ended up being two life sentences served consecutively rather than concurrently—McKinney was asked if he'd like to make a statement.

"I don't know what to say other than I am sorry to the entire Shepard family," he almost shrugged. "There won't be a day that goes by that I won't be ashamed for what I did."

His statement seemed like such a woefully inadequate response to all that he had done to tear my family apart. He exhibited no remorse. By that point, I guess, I couldn't have expected any more from him. But I wanted so desperately to let him, his attorneys, the jurors, and all the journalists in the room know just how much Matt meant to us. Thankfully, Dennis knew just what to say in his statement to the court:

Your Honor, members of the jury, Mr. Rerucha:

I would like to begin my statement by addressing the jury. Ladies and gentlemen, a terrible crime was committed in Laramie thirteen months ago. Because of that crime, the reputation of the city of Laramie, the University of Wyoming, and the state of Wyoming became synonymous with gay bashing, hate crimes, and brutality. While some of this reputation may be deserved, it was blown out of proportion by our friends in the media. Yesterday you, the jury, showed the world that Wyoming and the city of Laramie will not tolerate hate crimes. Yes, this was a hate crime, pure and simple, with the added ingredient of robbery. My son Matthew paid a terrible price to open the eyes of all of us who live in Wyoming, the United States, and the world to the unjust and unnecessary fears, discrimination, and intolerance that members of the gay community face every day. Yesterday's decision by you showed true courage and made a statement. That statement is that Wyoming is the Equality State; that Wyoming will not tolerate discrimination based on sexual orientation; that violence is not the solution. Ladies and gentlemen, you have the respect and admiration of Matthew's family and friends and of countless strangers around the world. Be proud of what you have accomplished. You may have prevented another family from losing a son or daughter.

Your Honor, I would also like to thank you for the dignity and grace with which this trial was conducted. Repeated attempts to distract the court from the true purpose of this trial failed because of your attentiveness, knowledge, and willingness to take a stand and make new law in the area of sexual orientation and the "gay panic" defense. By doing so you have emphasized that Matthew was a human being with all the rights and responsibilities and protections of any citizen of Wyoming.

Mr. Rerucha took the oath of office as any prosecuting attorney to protect the rights of the citizens of Albany County as mandated by the laws of the state of Wyoming, regardless of his personal feelings and beliefs. At no time did Mr. Rerucha make any decision on the outcome of this case without the permission of Judy and me. It was our decision to take this case to trial, just as it was our decision to accept the plea bargain today and the earlier plea bargain of Mr. Henderson. A trial was necessary to show that this was a hate crime and not just a robbery gone bad. If we had sought a plea bargain earlier, the facts of this case would not have been known and the question would always be present that we had something to hide. In addition, this trial was necessary to help provide some closure to the citizens of Laramie, Albany County, and the state. I find it intolerable that the priests of the Catholic Church and Newman Center would attempt to influence the jury, the prosecution, and the outcome of this trial by the castigation and persecution of Mr. Rerucha and his family in his private life, by their newspaper advertisements, and by their presence in the courtroom. I find it difficult to believe that they speak for all Catholics. If the leaders of the churches want to comment as private citizens, that is one thing. If they say that they represent the beliefs of their church, that is another. This country was founded on separation of church and state. The Catholic Church has stepped over the line and has become a political group with its own agenda. If that be the case, treat them as a political group and eliminate their privileges as a religious organization.

My son Matthew did not look like a winner. After all, he was small for his age—weighing, at the most, 110 pounds, and standing only five feet two inches tall. He was rather uncoordinated and wore braces from the age of thirteen until the day he died. However, in his all too brief life, he proved that he was a winner. My son—a gentle, caring soul—proved that he was as tough as, if not tougher than, anyone I have ever heard of or known. On October 6, 1998, my son tried to show the world that he could win again. On October 12, 1998, my firstborn son—and my hero—lost. On October 12, my firstborn son—and my hero—died fifty days before his twenty-second birthday. He died quietly, surrounded by family and friends, with his mother and brother holding his hand. All that I have now are the memories.

It's hard to put into words how much Matt meant to family and friends and how much they meant to him. Everyone wanted him to succeed because he tried so hard. The spark that he provided to people had to be experienced. He simply made everyone feel better about themselves. Family and friends were his focus. He knew that he always had their support for anything that he wanted to try.

Matt's gift was people. He loved being with people, helping people, and making others feel good. The hope of a better world free of harassment and discrimination because a person was different kept him motivated. All his life he felt the stabs of discrimination. Because of that he was sensitive to other people's feelings. He was naive to the extent that, regardless of the wrongs people did to him, he still had faith that they would change and become "nice." Matt trusted people, perhaps too much. Violence was not a part of his life until his senior year in high school. He would walk into a fight and break it up. He was the perfect negotiator. He could get two people talking to each other again as no one else could.

Matt loved people and he trusted them. He could never understand how one person could hurt another, physically or verbally. They would hurt him, and he would give them another chance. This quality of seeing only good gave him friends around the world. He didn't see race, intelligence, sex, religion, or the hundred other things that people use to make choices about people. All he saw was the person. All he wanted was to make another person his friend. All he wanted was to make another person feel good. All he wanted was to be accepted as an equal.

What did Matt's friends think of him? Fifteen of his friends from high school in Switzerland, as well as his high school adviser, joined hundreds of others at his memorial services. They left college, fought a blizzard, and came together one more time to say good-bye to Matt. Men and women coming from different countries, cultures, and religions thought enough of my son to drop every-thing and come to Wyoming—most of them for the first time. That's why this Wyoming country boy wanted to major in foreign relations and languages. He wanted to continue making friends and at the same time help others. He wanted to make a difference. Did he? You tell me.

I loved my son and, as can be seen throughout this statement, was proud of him. He was not my gay son. He was my son who happened to be gay. He was a good-looking, intelligent, caring person. There were the usual arguments, and at times he was a real pain in the butt. I felt the regrets of a father when he realizes that his son is not a star athlete. But it was replaced by greater pride when I saw him on the stage. The hours that he spent learning his parts, working behind the scenes, and helping others made me realize that he was actually an excellent athlete—in a more dynamic way—because of the different types of physical and mental conditioning required by ac-tors. To this day I have never figured out how he was able to spend all those hours at the theater, during the school year, and still have good grades.

Because my job involved lots of travel, I never had the

same give-and-take with Matt that Judy had. Our relationship at times was strained. But whenever he had problems we talked. For example, he was unsure about revealing to me that he was gay. He was afraid that I would reject him immediately, so it took him a while to tell me. By that time, his mother and brother had already been told. One day he said that he had something to say. I could see that he was nervous, so I asked him if everything was all right. Matt took a deep breath and told me that he was gay. Then he waited for my reaction. I still remember his surprise when I said, "Yeah, okay, but what's the point of the conversation?" Then everything was okay. We went back to a father and son who loved each other and respected the beliefs of the other. We were father and son, but we were also friends.

How do I talk about the loss that I feel every time I think about Matt? How can I describe the empty pit in my heart and mind when I think about all the problems that were put in Matt's way that he overcame? No one can understand the sense of pride and accomplishment that I felt every time he reached the mountaintop of another obstacle. No one, including myself, will ever know the frustration and agony that others put him through because he was different. How many people could be given the problems that Matt was presented with and still succeed as he did? How many would continue to smile—at least on the outside—while crying on the inside to keep other people from feeling bad?

I now feel very fortunate that I was able to spend some private time with Matt last summer during my vacation from Saudi Arabia. We sat and talked. I told Matt that he was my hero and that he was the toughest man that I had ever known. When I said that, I bowed down to him out of respect for his ability to continue to smile and keep a positive attitude during all the trials and tribulations that he had gone through. He just laughed. I also told him how proud I was because of what he had accomplished and what he was trying to accomplish. The last thing I said to Matt was that I loved him, and he said he loved me. That was the last private conversation I ever had with him.

Impact on my life? My life will never be the same. I miss Matt terribly. I think about him all the time—at odd moments when some little thing reminds me of him; when I walk by the refrigerator and see the pictures of him and his brother that we've always kept on the door; at special times of the year, like the first day of classes at UW or opening day of sage chicken hunting. I keep wondering almost the same thing that I did when I first saw him in the hospital. What would he have become? How would he have changed his piece of the world to make it better?

Impact on my life? I feel a tremendous sense of guilt. Why wasn't I there when he needed me most? Why didn't

I spend more time with him? Why didn't I try to find another type of profession so that I could have been available to spend more time with him as he grew up? What could I have done to be a better father and friend? How do I get an answer to those questions now? The only one who can answer them is Matt. These questions will be with me for the rest of my life. What makes it worse for me is knowing that his mother and brother will have similar unanswered questions.

Impact on my life? In addition to losing my son, I lost my father on November 4, 1998. The stress of the entire affair was too much for him. Dad watched Matt grow up. He taught him how to hunt, fish, camp, ride horses, and love the state of Wyoming. Matt, Logan, Dad, and I would spend two to three weeks camping in the mountains at different times of the year—to hunt, to fish, and to goof off. Matt learned to cook over an open fire, tell fishing stories about the one that got away, and to drive a truck from my father. Three weeks before Matt went to the Fireside Bar for the last time, my parents saw Matt in Laramie. In addition, my father tried calling Matt the night that he was beaten but received no answer. He never got over the guilt of not trying earlier. The additional strain of the hospital vigil, being in the hospital room with Matt when he died, the funeral services with all the media attention and the protesters, and helping Judy and me clean out Matt's apartment in Laramie a few days later was too much.

Three weeks after Matt's death, Dad died. Dad told me after the funeral that he never expected to outlive Matt. The stress and the grief were just too much for him.

Impact on my life? How can my life ever be the same again? When Matt was little, I used to take showers with him, just to teach him not to be scared of the water. Later, Matt helped me do the same thing with Logan. Anyway, Matt and I would be in the shower spitting mouthfuls of water at each other or at his mother, if he could convince her to come into the bathroom. Then he would laugh and laugh. We would sing in the showers. I taught him the songs, "Row, Row, Row Your Boat"; both "Brother John" and its French version, "Frère Jacques"; and "Twinkle, Twinkle, Little Star." Matt would sing loud and clear. Now, that voice is silent, the boat has sunk, Jacques is no longer *frère*, and the little star no longer twinkles.

Matt officially died at 12:53 a.m. on Monday, October 12, 1998, in a hospital in Fort Collins, Colorado. He actually died on the outskirts of Laramie, tied to a fence that Wednesday before, when you beat him. You, Mr. McKinney, with your friend Mr. Henderson, killed my son.

By the end of the beating, his body was just trying to survive. You left him out there by himself, but he wasn't alone. There were his lifelong friends with him—friends that he had grown up with. You're probably wondering who these friends were. First, he had the beautiful night sky with the same stars and moon that we used to look at through the telescope. Then, he had the daylight and the sun to shine on him one more time—one more cool, wonderful autumn day in Wyoming. His last day alive in Wyoming. His last day alive in the state that he always proudly called home. And through it all he was breathing in for the last time the smell of Wyoming sagebrush and the scent of pine trees from the snowy range. He heard the wind—the ever-present Wyoming wind—for the last time. He had one more friend with him. One he grew to know through his time in Sunday school and as an acolyte at St. Mark's in Casper as well as through his visits to St. Matthew's in Laramie. He had God. I feel better knowing he wasn't alone.

Matt became a symbol—some say a martyr, putting a boy-next-door face on hate crimes. That's fine with me. Matt would be thrilled if his death would help others. On the other hand, your agreement to life without parole has taken yourself out of the spotlight and out of the public eye. It means no drawn-out appeals process, no chance of walking away free due to a technicality, and no chance of a lighter sentence due to a "merciful" jury. Best of all, you won't be a symbol. No years of publicity, no chance of communication, no nothing—just a miserable future and a more miserable end. It works for me.

My son was taught to look at all sides of an issue before making a decision or taking a stand. He learned this early when he was helping various political candidates while in grade school and junior high. When he did take a stand, it was based on his best judgment. Such a stand cost him his life when he quietly let it be known that he was gay. He didn't advertise it, but he didn't back away from the issue either. For that I'll always be proud of him. He showed me that he was a lot more courageous than most people, including myself. Matt knew that there were dangers to being gay, but he accepted that and wanted to just get on with his life and his ambition of helping others.

Matt's beating, hospitalization, and funeral focused worldwide attention on hate. Good is coming out of evil. People have said, "Enough is enough." You screwed up, Mr. McKinney. You made the world realize that a person's lifestyle is not a reason for discrimination, intolerance, persecution, and violence. This is not the 1920s, '30s, and '40s of Nazi Germany. My son died because of your ignorance and intolerance. I can't bring him back. But I can do my best to see that this never, ever happens to another person or another family again. As I mentioned earlier, my son has become a symbol—a symbol against hate and people like you; a symbol for encouraging respect for individuality; for appreciating that someone is different; for tolerance. I miss my son, but I'm proud to be able to say that he is my son.

Mr. McKinney, one final comment before I sit, and this is the reason that I stand before you now. At no time since Matt was found at the fence and taken to the hospital have Judy and I made any statements about our beliefs concerning the death penalty. We felt that that would be an undue influence on any prospective juror. Judy has been quoted by some right-wing groups as being against the death penalty. It has been stated that Matt was against the death penalty. Both of these statements are wrong. We have held family discussions and talked about the death penalty. For example, he and I discussed the horrible death of James Byrd Jr., in Jasper, Texas. It was his opinion that the death penalty should be sought and that no expense should be spared to bring those responsible for this murder to justice. Little did we know that the same response would come involving Matt. I, too, believe in the death penalty. I would like nothing better than to see you die, Mr. McKinney. However, this is the time to begin the healing process. To show mercy to someone who refused to show any mercy. To use this as the first step in my own closure about losing Matt. Mr. McKinney, I am not doing this because of your family. I am definitely not doing this because of the crass and unwarranted pressures put on by the religious community. If anything, that hardens my resolve to see you die. Mr. McKinney, I'm going to grant you life, as hard as that is for me to do, because of Matthew. Every time you celebrate Christmas, a birthday, or the Fourth of July, remember that Matt isn't. Every time that you wake up in that prison cell, remember that you had the opportunity and the ability to stop your actions that night. Every time that you see your cellmate, remember that you had a choice, and now you are living that choice. You robbed me of something very precious, and I will never forgive you for that. Mr. McKinney, I give you life in the memory of one who no longer lives. May you have a long life, and may you thank Matthew every day for it.

Your Honor, members of the jury, Mr. Rerucha, thank you.

I'VE ALWAYS CONSIDERED myself pretty politically aware. Since I'd known that Matt was gay, I did my best to stay up-to-date on the issues that I considered of gay interest—things like gay marriage and gays in the military. But it wasn't until the day of Matt's memorial service that I had ever heard of the Human Rights Campaign (HRC), and that was only because a middle-aged man I'd never seen before introduced himself and handed me what appeared to be a business card. At the time, I thought, "A business card? Really?" I couldn't believe the guy's gall and couldn't help but exchange a "can you believe this guy?" glance with Dennis when he handed the card to me. At that point in the day, I couldn't begin to imagine what kind of business he was hoping to conduct with me, but it seemed pretty clear that he was hoping to capitalize on my family's pain.

Later that night, back at the hotel, I took the business card out of my purse and took a closer look at it. It identified the man as Dennis Dougherty, a Denver resident and member of the Washington, D.C.–based HRC. On the back of the card, he'd scrawled a note: "My mother and I have just donated ten thousand dollars to HRC in Matthew's name."

I was so moved by Dennis Dougherty's graciousness—and embarrassed enough by my rush to judgment at the church—that I held on to his card. A month or so later, after my Dennis returned to Saudi Arabia and I was living alone in Wyoming, I called Dennis Dougherty to talk with him more about his work with HRC.

By this time it had become clear that it was going to largely be up to me to figure out how my family and the foundation that the three of us had formed in Matt's memory could harness the attention that had been directed our way. I needed to try and refocus it on the organizations that were already fighting to make sure there was never another murder like Matt's. But what were those organizations? What kinds of work were they doing? And, perhaps more important, how could the Matthew Shepard Foundation aid in their efforts?

Clearly I had my work cut out for me, and I understood that I needed to be in Wyoming, even if it meant that I was going to be there all by myself.

Unfortunately, at that point I didn't really feel like I could turn to any of my longtime Casper friends for help. Aside from a few very notable exceptions, my relationships with folks back home had become strained after we moved to Saudi Arabia. Every time I returned home, it seemed like we had less in common and, consequently, less to talk about. They always asked what it was like to live in Saudi Arabia, but I never could find the words to explain how different it was from Wyoming or what it was really like to live there. So I'd tell them what I thought they wanted to hear—like how hot it got and whether I had to change the way I dressed. My friendships suffered as a result. It wasn't anybody's fault—mine or theirs. It was just that, over the years, we seemed to have less in common and naturally grew apart. We'd always catch up when I was back in town, asking each other courteous questions. But Matt's death made small talk uncomfortable and forced conversations only more forced and uncomfortable. Our children were one of the last things I had in common with most of my old Casper friends, and now, when we ran into each other, it seemed like they were either afraid to bring up my kids or scared that if they did it would send me careening off track. I suppose I understand where my friends were coming from, and I can imagine that I would have been equally uncomfortable if I were in their place. Nevertheless, I didn't feel like I could turn to some of the people who used to know me best because it was too uncomfortable, for all parties, for me to be upfront about the woman I needed to become. I had to talk about my son, and I couldn't pretend that he hadn't been murdered. If I didn't speak up, I feared, I'd miss my one shot at making something—anything, really—positive come out of Matt's murder.

Looking back on it now, I see that my decision to call Dennis Dougherty on one of those cold and lonely days in Wyoming was one of my first attempts at finding my new voice. I wanted him to tell me about the Human Rights Campaign and its work, and he explained—in strokes broad enough for a beginning activist like me to understand—that HRC was the largest civil rights organization focused on achieving equality for gay, lesbian, bisexual, and transgender Americans. He then invited me to be his guest at one of the group's fund-raising dinners in Denver, explaining that going to the event would be the best way for me to truly understand HRC's mission and the importance of the group's work.

When I told my Dennis about the dinner, he encouraged me to go, saying that the folks from HRC might be able to help us better hone our plans for the Matthew Shepard Foundation. I was a little more skeptical though. As genuine as I understood Dennis Dougherty's invitation to be, I was fearful that HRC would get more out of me than I'd be able to get out of the organization. Ever since Matt's death I'd felt like everybody in the media wanted a piece of me, and I figured the folks at HRC might only be inviting me to the dinner so they could somehow publicize that I was there and raise more money at their fund-raising dinner than usual. It makes me laugh today to think that I was ever so fearful of such a fund-raising tactic—especially because I'm now more than happy to lend my name to help raise money for a worthwhile cause. But I was a different woman back then, and after what had been taken from me, I had a lot to learn about trust.

Despite my fear, I did end up joining Dennis Dougherty at the HRC dinner. I have no idea whether he publicized that I'd be there, although, given my reluctance to commit to the affair, it was probably close to impossible for him to do so. But from what I could tell from the size of the crowd in the ballroom of that Denver hotel that night, HRC didn't need my help to sell tickets.

In all honesty, though, I probably shouldn't have gone that night. It was simply too much so soon after Matt's death. The news of Matt's murder hit close to home for people in Denver, both because the city is so close to Wyoming and because Matt had lived there for a time. When I walked into the ballroom that night, and especially after the MC announced from the podium that I was there, everybody's fear and anger—coupled with what I could tell was respect for what my family was trying to do with the foundation—was overwhelming. It was extremely hard to feel everybody else's pain when I hadn't yet figured out how to handle my own grief.

Nevertheless, when Dennis Dougherty suggested that I meet Elizabeth Birch, who was then HRC's executive director, it wasn't long before I was on a plane to Washington, D.C., to do just that.

I can honestly say that Elizabeth is like no woman I've ever met. A mother herself, with boy and girl twins, she has the warmest embrace and the most soothing voice. Elizabeth uses both with amazing expertise, whether it's to talk with a new friend, to put a loved one at ease, or to get what she wants. And I soon learned that Elizabeth was especially adept at getting what she wanted. A former corporate attorney for Apple Computer, she had been HRC's executive director for four years at that point, and in that time the group had ballooned in size and influence.

When we met that morning in early 1999, Elizabeth wanted two things: to let me know that she would be a compassionate, empathetic, and understanding friend if I needed one, and to convince me of my potential as an activist. She knocked her first task out of the park, and she has since become one of my closest and dearest friends. I wasn't immediately convinced by her second point, though. Although I agreed with her that I had a once-in-a-lifetime chance—a national platform, if you will—to speak out in favor of equal rights for gay men and lesbians, as well as the transgendered community. I wasn't sure that I had a spokeswoman in me. Up until that point, I had envisioned myself growing into more of a behind-the-scenes kind of activist, supporting the work of national groups like HRC.

"But you're the one people want to hear from, whether you like it or not," Elizabeth pressed, as she promised to teach me about the issues and help me learn to speak about them effectively and with authority.

She and David Smith, who was HRC's director of communications at the time and now works as the group's vice president of programs, were the first to fully educate me about the merits of hate-crimes laws. The idea behind these laws was that someone who committed a crime that was motivated by the victim's perceived difference—whether it be race, religion, sexual orientation, or physical handicap—would face a harsher penalty upon conviction.

It was an issue that had been hotly debated across the country since Matt had been murdered, and one I'd chosen to steer clear of until I was more fully informed. The argument of those who are opposed to hate-crimes laws is that "any crime is a hate crime." But Elizabeth and David very convincingly explained to me that while random acts of violence against another person are always tragic events, violent crimes based on prejudice have a much stronger impact because the motive for crime is to terrorize an entire community. Hate crimes like the one committed against Matt, they explained, are often more violent because the perpetrator is trying to send a message that the victim—whether he or she is black, gay, transgender, or Jewish—will not be tolerated.

Underscoring their point, Elizabeth and David pointed to statistics that showed that the number of hate crimes almost always spiked following periods of high visibility and celebration for a minority group, whether it was the Million Man March for African American men or any of the hundreds of gay pride parades held around the country every summer.

A federal hate-crimes law had been in place for nearly thirty years by the time Matt was killed. But it didn't (and, as I write this, still doesn't) include protections based on sexual orientation—even though those crimes constitute nearly 16 percent of all bias-based crimes. And although there are forty-five states with hate-crimes laws on the books, only thirty-one of them included protections based on a victim's real or perceived sexual orientation. Another five states, Wyoming among them, had no hate-crimes law whatsoever.

Now I agree with those people who say that it's naive to think hate-crimes laws will stop all bias-based crimes. A dyed-in-the-wool and determined bigot isn't about to log onto the Internet to check state or federal statutes before bashing someone's head in. But what hate-crimes laws will do is make it easier to prosecute those people who commit hate crimes—and more effectively ensure that they'll serve sentences (and full sentences at that) to fit.

More important, well-written and judicially enforced hate-crimes laws have the potential of nipping bias in the bud—before it has the chance to blossom into the kind of full-blown hatred that possessed Henderson and McKinney. Kids who are caught spray painting "Fag" on a neighbor's home might, in addition to the standard sentence of a fine and probation, be required by the court to take diversity training courses. If a class like that can open only one young person's eyes to the idea of accepting other people in spite of their differences, then in my opinion the program is a smashing success.

But all these statistics and arguments in favor of hate-crimes laws didn't answer my bigger question: What, if anything, can I do to help? So Elizabeth decided to throw me headfirst into the deep end of the pool of activism, asking me to join her, U.S. Rep. Sheila Jackson Lee of Texas, and a nephew of James Byrd Jr., a recent victim of a heinous racial hate crime in Texas, at the National Press Club to speak in favor of a bill before Congress that would add protections based on sexual orientation to the federal hate-crimes law.

Like most people who fall under Elizabeth's nurturing spell, I did what she asked. So that's how, on March 23, 1999, just barely more than five months after Matt had passed, I ended up giving my first press conference. I should have guessed—based on the experience I had standing next to Dennis when he addressed the media on the day of Matt's memorial service—what I was in for at the National Press Club. But when I got up at the front of the room and started to talk publicly about Matt for the first time, I started to cry. When I heard the sea of cameras start to click as my eyes began to tear up, I felt the same thing as when I had stood next to Dennis. It seemed like the reporters were only there to see me cry, that they didn't give a damn about what I had to say.

News reports from the event, including the following wire report, only confirmed my suspicion of the press:

" 'Hate crimes are perpetrated against a group of people, not an individual,' Shepard told reporters, choking back tears. 'It is a form of domestic terrorism. On behalf of my family, I call on the Congress of the United States to pass this legislation right away.' "

Even though the bulk of what I had to say made it into the wire report, all I could see were those six words: "Shepard told reporters, choking back tears." It frustrated me to no end that I came across as weak—little more than a mourning mother—when I had so many important things to say.

Still, encouraged by Elizabeth and a number of other activists who quickly became my friends (from groups such as the Gay & Lesbian Alliance Against Defamation; Parents, Families and Friends of Lesbians and Gays; and the Gay, Lesbian and Straight Education Network), I continued to speak out, even taping public service announcements to decry hate speech and bullying in schools.

Immediately following Aaron McKinney's sentencing, Dennis and I flew back to Washington, D.C., to lobby in favor of the hate-crimes bill before Congress. We met with White House chief of staff John Podesta, who assured us that President Clinton and Vice President Gore were wholeheartedly behind the proposal, and we met with Attorney General Janet Reno, who told us that the Justice Department supported it as well. Then we gave a press conference with two Republican senators, Gordon Smith of Oregon and Jim Jeffords of Vermont, to demonstrate that support for the bill crossed party lines. Senator Smith, who is Mormon but had always been one of the biggest supporters of hate-crimes protections on Capitol Hill (until he lost his bid for reelection in 2008), addressed head-on the concern of some religious conservatives that support for the bill was somehow endorsing so-called sinful behaviors. "If you want to talk with me about sin, go with me to church," he said. "If you want to talk about public policy, then go with me to the U.S. Senate. That's the separation of church and state."

Still, the hate-crimes bill didn't make it out of the Republican-controlled Congress that time, and more than ten years since Matt's death, it still has yet to be passed. The closest we've come was in 2007, when the proposal, which was by that time renamed the Matthew Shepard Act at the request of Senators Kennedy and Smith, was attached as an amendment to a defense reauthorization bill and passed the Senate. But that bill got tripped up by politics related to the Iraq War, and the hate-crimes provision was dropped before the reauthorization bill made it to President Bush's desk. But I'm increasingly optimistic after the election of Barack Obama. Before he became president, Obama promised to sign the Matthew Shepard Act into law when it reaches his desk, and as I write this chapter Congress is again debating the bill.

IF THERE WAS ONE THING that Dennis and I had figured out in the year after Matt had died—a year in which we both, for the most part, did our best to dodge the press—it was that we'd have to address the mounting media requests, sooner rather than later, if we ever wanted our lives to get back somewhere close to normal. Don't get me wrong; it wasn't that either of us was being chased by paparazzi hungry for information about anything we were doing. But the American public had identified so much with the picture of Matt plastered on newspapers across the country after his death, that there was a real desire for more information about who our son really was. As uncomfortable as both Dennis and I were when it came to talking publicly—and as sensitive and as private as our memories of Matt were to us—we were more concerned about what the press would write about our son if we didn't tell them who he really was. Early reports almost deified Matt, presenting him as a martyr of sorts—a kid who could do no wrong who had been crucified for being gay. But like any living human, Matt was far from a saint. Dennis and I feared that the media risked muddying the real lesson we hoped people would take away—that Matt's murder wasn't horrific because it ended an angelic life but because it ended a very human life riddled with all the complexities and contradictions each of us face.

We also learned that the public's interest in Matt's life and in his attack wasn't easily satiated. Even after high-profile interviews like those with Katie Couric, *Vanity Fair*, and *People*, the e-mails, cards, and letters—some addressed only to "The Shepard Family, Wyoming"—kept coming.

After McKinney's sentencing and after Dennis's and my trip to lobby on behalf of the hate-crimes bill, Dennis returned to Saudi Arabia. For the first time, I had a chance to start sifting through the tens of thousands of messages people had left for us in the year since Matt's murder. Many of them were simple, yet heartfelt, notes of condolence. But many others were from people who wanted to share their own stories. There were letters from parents who had struggled with coming to terms with their child's sexual orientation until they heard Dennis and I express our love for Matt, notes from kids who were thrown out of the house after coming out of the closet to their folks, and cards from straight students who'd organized Gay-Straight Alliance groups at their high schools and colleges in response to Matt's murder.

Reading through stacks of those letters in one sitting was emotionally exhausting—not unlike when I was first faced with everyone's pain at that HRC dinner in Denver. But reading what others wrote was cathartic, too. I kept going back, finding myself continuously moved and inspired. Eventually, it occurred to me that it wasn't so much the details of Matt's life, or even the tragedy of his death, that drove many of these individuals to write. For most of them, it was the fact that my family was the first they could identify with. Many of the parents writing were in the same position I'd been in fifteen years earlier, when I first considered that my little boy might be gay but didn't know where to turn for more information. Many of the kids who were writing, I imagined, were in the same place Matt must have been when he first realized he was somehow "different" but was too afraid to put words to that difference for fear that he'd be alienated from his friends and family.

It was by reading those cards and letters—and with the guidance of new friends like Elizabeth Birch—that Dennis and I gained a clearer understanding of what the mission of the Matthew Shepard Foundation needed to be. It wouldn't be about tolerance, since you tolerate bad hair days, not people. It needed to be about accepting people for who they are. We also wanted visibility and awareness: to let folks like the thousands who had written Dennis and me know that they weren't alone. Above all else, the foundation needed to be about respect and compassion for, and understanding of, other people's difficulties, differences, and similarities.

Ultimately, our family settled on three areas of focus for the foundation:

1. Erase Hate: Educating society about all aspects of hate—whether it's based on race, ethnicity, gender, or sexual orientation.

2. Lesbian, Gay, Bisexual, and Transgender Equality: This is the work that would have been the closest to Matt's heart and includes supporting groups like the Human Rights Campaign in their fight for marriage equality,

for employment nondiscrimination laws, and for an end to the military's ban on openly gay service members.

3. Put Children First: The goal here is to educate the public on the needs of gay and lesbian youth. Five years ago, the average age of gay teens coming out of the closet was nineteen. Today it's fourteen. As a result, there are more openly gay teens facing discrimination in school and/or in their homes.

Having determined this mission, a bigger question remained: How was I going to actually get out in public and advocate these issues? I'd tried speaking at press conferences and granting interviews to various journalists, but in both of those cases my message ended up being filtered before it actually made it to my intended audience. I doubted if the press would ever be able to get past the point of presenting me as a sorrowful mother. Of course I was still grieving, but the issues that I wanted the Matthew Shepard Foundation to focus on were about so much more than my tragedy—even more than what my family had been through. So in order to make this foundation a worthwhile venture, I knew I'd need to get my message across without focusing solely on my own story.

In 2000 one of my nieces had a friend who worked for Keppler Speakers bureau and she suggested signing up with them. She and her friend thought that giving speeches on college campuses and to corporate diversity groups would not only be a fantastic way to raise money for the foundation but would also promote my unfiltered message to the world. I couldn't agree with their suggestion more, but I wasn't confident I would make a compelling public speaker. I was scared to death even after I eventually agreed to give the idea a chance by addressing a group of students at the University of Maine at Orono. Public speaking wasn't something I ever wanted to do. But it turned out that I really didn't have to do "public speaking." I just had to tell my story.

Now I begin almost all the speeches I give with the victim's impact statement I first read at Henderson's sentencing. I do so partly to remind the audience of what happened to my son—to my family—in October 1998. I also remind the audience that my son was killed because two men learned that it was okay to hate.

"Somehow and somewhere they received the message that the lives of 'the others' are not as worthy of respect, dignity, and honor as the lives of 'us,'" I read. "They were given the impression that society condones or is at least indifferent to violence against 'the others.'"

Then, as an introduction to my overall civil-rights campaign, I use an acronym that a friend once shared with me:

"We have become a SIC society: silent, indifferent, and complacent," I say. "For all who ask what they can do for Matt and for all the other victims of hate—my answer is to educate and bring understanding where you see hate and ignorance, bring light where you see darkness, bring freedom where there is fear, and begin to heal."

That, in essence, is my message today: We, as Americans, need to learn from the past but focus on the future; we need to fight discrimination by becoming informed, active, and vocal citizens.

To date, I've spoken to more than a million people. Requests for information about Matt keep coming. Curiosity that was first prompted by the news following the attack, and subsequently Henderson's and McKinney's sentencing, is now stoked by movies on MTV and NBC and, of course, by Moisés Kaufman's amazing play *The Laramie Project*, which has now been produced thousands of times—in big-city theaters, high school auditoriums, and churches—and has been adapted into a movie by HBO.

More than a decade after my son's death, it's the interest in his life that keeps me going. It's also what keeps me thousands of miles away from my husband, who still works in Saudi Arabia, and has me living out of a suitcase at least two-thirds of the year. It's why I wanted to write this book.

I wanted to make sure the truth was told. There are so many misconceptions about Matt and our family, as a result of the news stories and, especially, as a result of the TV movies, including NBC's *The Matthew Shepard Story*, starring Stockard Channing and Sam Waterston. I was flattered by Channing's portrayal of me (she won an Emmy and a Screen Actors Guild Award for it), but the movie was filled with inaccuracies—everything from the way Matt came out of the closet to how McKinney's plea agreement was negotiated.

I also wanted to reach out to parents of gay children—regardless of whether they accept their child's sexual orientation—to tell them the story of a gay son and his family who loved one another so much. I want to connect with people who live in places where I'm not invited to speak. There are still nineteen states where crimes motivated by the victim's sexual orientation, actual or perceived, are not considered hate crimes; and there are thirty states where it's still okay to fire people because of their sexual orientation.

Conflicting schedules and distance have cut down on the number of times Dennis, Logan, and I can be together these days. But when we are, Matt's always a part of those gatherings. On every Christmas we still hang the stocking that his grandmother made for him as a newborn. Memories of my Matt are always in my thoughts. Until the hatred and ignorance that cut his life short are stemmed—through a combination of legal protections—we will continue to do everything we can to keep his story in society's greater consciousness as well.

Epilogue

Today, after every speech I make, I open up the floor to questions and try to answer whatever anyone wants to ask. What I hear most often is, "How do you do it?" As many times as that question comes up, I'm never sure how to respond. Part of the problem, I think, is that people assume that I've somehow found a way, for the purposes of a speech or for a newspaper interview, to tap into the pain and torture of Matt's murder and then return to my everyday life unscathed. The question is always posed as if I have some sort of superhuman power or something. *How do you do it?*

But the truth is that, more than a decade after losing Matt, I still haven't come to terms with his death, and I don't want to. The only way I've been able to get through the hundreds of speeches and interviews over the past ten years is the same way I was able to get through Henderson's and McKinney's trials in 1999—by never ever going to that place in my head if I can help it. I've never visited the spot on the east side of

Laramie where Henderson and McKinney tied Matt to that fence to die, and eight years had to pass before I could bring myself to watch a production of *The Laramie Project*, which was performed as part of a fund-raiser for the foundation, in New York City, on what would have been Matt's thirtieth birthday.

So I'm not superhuman. And the real answer to the question of how I do it is one of mind over matter. The speeches and interviews I give are my equivalent of walking over hot coals. I race over my emotions before they have a chance to burn me.

But having said that, I've learned a thing or two from the advice I've been giving to those millions of people during these past ten years. I understand that not only do I need to learn from the past but I have to pay attention to the future. For me, the future lies in continuing to focus on the goals of the Matthew Shepard Foundation.

As I mentioned earlier, the goals of the foundation are to erase hate, ensure equality, and put youth first. Our overall goal is to, "Replace hate with understanding, compassion, and acceptance." I encourage everyone to log onto the foundation's Web site, matthewshepard.org, where you can not only see photographs of Matt and our family as he was growing up, but you can find a list of all the different things you can do to help the foundation make a difference in achieving these goals.

Dennis and I keep promising each other that there will come a time when the Matthew Shepard Foundation will become irrelevant, when it's inconceivable that gay people were ever considered anything other than vital to what makes our world wonderful. When I really think about it, that's the future I'm focused on.

Dennis and I will eventually live together in Casper again, and our days will be filled with friends, family, and our memories of Matt. At night, after everyone's gone home, the two of us will sit in the living room, warmed by the light of the same setting sun and invigorated by the sound of the same whipping wind that's kept my family coming back to Wyoming all these years. If you take nothing else away from my story, please take away the fact that we loved Matt for Matt's sake. As Dennis once said in a speech he gave in Washington, D.C., and I paraphrase here: Matt was not our gay son; Matt was our son who happened to be gay.

Printed in the United States
by Baker & Taylor Publisher Services